# PERSIAN
## VOCABULARY

# ENGLISH-PERSIAN

The most useful words
To expand your lexicon and sharpen
your language skills

## 5000 words

# Persian vocabulary for English speakers - 5000 words

By Andrey Taranov

T&P Books vocabularies are intended for helping you learn, memorize and review foreign words. The dictionary is divided into themes, covering all major spheres of everyday activities, business, science, culture, etc.

The process of learning words using T&P Books' theme-based dictionaries gives you the following advantages:

- Correctly grouped source information predetermines success at subsequent stages of word memorization
- Availability of words derived from the same root allowing memorization of word units (rather than separate words)
- Small units of words facilitate the process of establishing associative links needed for consolidation of vocabulary
- Level of language knowledge can be estimated by the number of learned words

T&P Books Publishing
www.tpbooks.com

ISBN: 978-1-78716-705-6

This book is also available in E-book formats.
Please visit www.tpbooks.com or the major online bookstores.

# PERSIAN VOCABULARY
## for English speakers

T&P Books vocabularies are intended to help you learn, memorize, and review foreign words. The vocabulary contains over 5000 commonly used words arranged thematically.

- Vocabulary contains the most commonly used words
- Recommended as an addition to any language course
- Meets the needs of beginners and advanced learners of foreign languages
- Convenient for daily use, revision sessions, and self-testing activities
- Allows you to assess your vocabulary

### Special features of the vocabulary

- Words are organized according to their meaning, not alphabetically
- Words are presented in three columns to facilitate the reviewing and self-testing processes
- Words in groups are divided into small blocks to facilitate the learning process
- The vocabulary offers a convenient and simple transcription of each foreign word

### The vocabulary has 155 topics including:

Basic Concepts, Numbers, Colors, Months, Seasons, Units of Measurement, Clothing & Accessories, Food & Nutrition, Restaurant, Family Members, Relatives, Character, Feelings, Emotions, Diseases, City, Town, Sightseeing, Shopping, Money, House, Home, Office, Working in the Office, Import & Export, Marketing, Job Search, Sports, Education, Computer, Internet, Tools, Nature, Countries, Nationalities and more ...

# T&P BOOKS' THEME-BASED DICTIONARIES

The Correct System for Memorizing Foreign Words

**Acquiring vocabulary is one of the most important elements of learning a foreign language, because words allow us to express our thoughts, ask questions, and provide answers. An inadequate vocabulary can impede communication with a foreigner and make it difficult to understand a book or movie well.**

The pace of activity in all spheres of modern life, including the learning of modern languages, has increased. Today, we need to memorize large amounts of information (grammar rules, foreign words, etc.) within a short period. However, this does not need to be difficult. All you need to do is to choose the right training materials, learn a few special techniques, and develop your individual training system.

Having a system is critical to the process of language learning. Many people fail to succeed in this regard; they cannot master a foreign language because they fail to follow a system comprised of selecting materials, organizing lessons, arranging new words to be learned, and so on. The lack of a system causes confusion and eventually, lowers self-confidence.

T&P Books' theme-based dictionaries can be included in the list of elements needed for creating an effective system for learning foreign words. These dictionaries were specially developed for learning purposes and are meant to help students effectively memorize words and expand their vocabulary.

### Generally speaking, the process of learning words consists of three main elements:

- Reception (creation or acquisition) of a training material, such as a word list
- Work aimed at memorizing new words
- Work aimed at reviewing the learned words, such as self-testing

All three elements are equally important since they determine the quality of work and the final result. All three processes require certain skills and a well-thought-out approach.

New words are often encountered quite randomly when learning a foreign language and it may be difficult to include them all in a unified list. As a result, these words remain written on scraps of paper, in book margins, textbooks, and so on. In order to systematize such words, we have to create and continually update a "book of new words." A paper notebook, a netbook, or a tablet PC can be used for these purposes.

This "book of new words" will be your personal, unique list of words. However, it will only contain the words that you came across during the learning process. For example, you might have written down the words "Sunday," "Tuesday," and "Friday." However, there are additional words for days of the week, for example, "Saturday," that are missing, and your list of words would be incomplete. Using a theme dictionary, in addition to the "book of new words," is a reasonable solution to this problem.

## The theme-based dictionary may serve as the basis for expanding your vocabulary.

It will be your big "book of new words" containing the most frequently used words of a foreign language already included. There are quite a few theme-based dictionaries available, and you should ensure that you make the right choice in order to get the maximum benefit from your purchase.

Therefore, we suggest using theme-based dictionaries from T&P Books Publishing as an aid to learning foreign words. Our books are specially developed for effective use in the sphere of vocabulary systematization, expansion and review.

Theme-based dictionaries are not a magical solution to learning new words. However, they can serve as your main database to aid foreign-language acquisition. Apart from theme dictionaries, you can have copybooks for writing down new words, flash cards, glossaries for various texts, as well as other resources; however, a good theme dictionary will always remain your primary collection of words.

## T&P Books' theme-based dictionaries are specialty books that contain the most frequently used words in a language.

The main characteristic of such dictionaries is the division of words into themes. For example, the *City* theme contains the words "street," "crossroads," "square," "fountain," and so on. The *Talking* theme might contain words like "to talk," "to ask," "question," and "answer".

All the words in a theme are divided into smaller units, each comprising 3–5 words. Such an arrangement improves the perception of words and makes the learning process less tiresome. Each unit contains a selection of words with similar meanings or identical roots. This allows you to learn words in small groups and establish other associative links that have a positive effect on memorization.

The words on each page are placed in three columns: a word in your native language, its translation, and its transcription. Such positioning allows for the use of techniques for effective memorization. After closing the translation column, you can flip through and review foreign words, and vice versa. "This is an easy and convenient method of review – one that we recommend you do often."

Our theme-based dictionaries contain transcriptions for all the foreign words. Unfortunately, none of the existing transcriptions are able to convey the exact nuances of foreign pronunciation. That is why we recommend using the transcriptions only as a supplementary learning aid. Correct pronunciation can only be acquired with the help of sound. Therefore our collection includes audio theme-based dictionaries.

## The process of learning words using T&P Books' theme-based dictionaries gives you the following advantages:

- You have correctly grouped source information, which predetermines your success at subsequent stages of word memorization
- Availability of words derived from the same root (lazy, lazily, lazybones), allowing you to memorize word units instead of separate words
- Small units of words facilitate the process of establishing associative links needed for consolidation of vocabulary
- You can estimate the number of learned words and hence your level of language knowledge
- The dictionary allows for the creation of an effective and high-quality revision process
- You can revise certain themes several times, modifying the revision methods and techniques
- Audio versions of the dictionaries help you to work out the pronunciation of words and develop your skills of auditory word perception

The T&P Books' theme-based dictionaries are offered in several variants differing in the number of words: 1.500, 3.000, 5.000, 7.000, and 9.000 words. There are also dictionaries containing 15,000 words for some language combinations. Your choice of dictionary will depend on your knowledge level and goals.

We sincerely believe that our dictionaries will become your trusty assistant in learning foreign languages and will allow you to easily acquire the necessary vocabulary.

# TABLE OF CONTENTS

**T&P Books' Theme-Based Dictionaries**     4
**Pronunciation guide**     13
**Abbreviations**     14

**BASIC CONCEPTS**     15
**Basic concepts. Part 1**     15

1. Pronouns     15
2. Greetings. Salutations. Farewells     15
3. How to address     16
4. Cardinal numbers. Part 1     16
5. Cardinal numbers. Part 2     17
6. Ordinal numbers     18
7. Numbers. Fractions     18
8. Numbers. Basic operations     18
9. Numbers. Miscellaneous     19
10. The most important verbs. Part 1     19
11. The most important verbs. Part 2     20
12. The most important verbs. Part 3     21
13. The most important verbs. Part 4     22
14. Colors     23
15. Questions     24
16. Prepositions     24
17. Function words. Adverbs. Part 1     25
18. Function words. Adverbs. Part 2     27

**Basic concepts. Part 2**     29

19. Weekdays     29
20. Hours. Day and night     29
21. Months. Seasons     30
22. Units of measurement     32
23. Containers     33

**HUMAN BEING**     35
**Human being. The body**     35

24. Head     35
25. Human body     36

## Clothing & Accessories                                         38

26. Outerwear. Coats                                              38
27. Men's & women's clothing                                      38
28. Clothing. Underwear                                           39
29. Headwear                                                      39
30. Footwear                                                      39
31. Personal accessories                                         40
32. Clothing. Miscellaneous                                      41
33. Personal care. Cosmetics                                     41
34. Watches. Clocks                                               42


## Food. Nutricion                                                44

35. Food                                                          44
36. Drinks                                                        46
37. Vegetables                                                    47
38. Fruits. Nuts                                                  47
39. Bread. Candy                                                  48
40. Cooked dishes                                                 49
41. Spices                                                        50
42. Meals                                                         50
43. Table setting                                                 51
44. Restaurant                                                    52


## Family, relatives and friends                                  53

45. Personal information. Forms                                   53
46. Family members. Relatives                                     53


## Medicine                                                        55

47. Diseases                                                       55
48. Symptoms. Treatments. Part 1                                  56
49. Symptoms. Treatments. Part 2                                  57
50. Symptoms. Treatments. Part 3                                  58
51. Doctors                                                       59
52. Medicine. Drugs. Accessories                                 59


## HUMAN HABITAT                                                   61
## City                                                           61

53. City. Life in the city                                        61
54. Urban institutions                                            62
55. Signs                                                         64
56. Urban transportation                                          65

| | | |
|---|---|---|
| 57. | Sightseeing | 66 |
| 58. | Shopping | 66 |
| 59. | Money | 67 |
| 60. | Post. Postal service | 68 |

**Dwelling. House. Home**     70

| | | |
|---|---|---|
| 61. | House. Electricity | 70 |
| 62. | Villa. Mansion | 70 |
| 63. | Apartment | 71 |
| 64. | Furniture. Interior | 71 |
| 65. | Bedding | 72 |
| 66. | Kitchen | 72 |
| 67. | Bathroom | 73 |
| 68. | Household appliances | 74 |

**HUMAN ACTIVITIES**     76
**Job. Business. Part 1**     76

| | | |
|---|---|---|
| 69. | Office. Working in the office | 76 |
| 70. | Business processes. Part 1 | 77 |
| 71. | Business processes. Part 2 | 78 |
| 72. | Production. Works | 79 |
| 73. | Contract. Agreement | 81 |
| 74. | Import & Export | 81 |
| 75. | Finances | 82 |
| 76. | Marketing | 83 |
| 77. | Advertising | 83 |
| 78. | Banking | 84 |
| 79. | Telephone. Phone conversation | 85 |
| 80. | Cell phone | 85 |
| 81. | Stationery | 86 |
| 82. | Kinds of business | 86 |

**Job. Business. Part 2**     89

| | | |
|---|---|---|
| 83. | Show. Exhibition | 89 |
| 84. | Science. Research. Scientists | 90 |

**Professions and occupations**     92

| | | |
|---|---|---|
| 85. | Job search. Dismissal | 92 |
| 86. | Business people | 92 |
| 87. | Service professions | 94 |
| 88. | Military professions and ranks | 94 |
| 89. | Officials. Priests | 95 |

| | | |
|---|---|---|
| 90. | Agricultural professions | 96 |
| 91. | Art professions | 96 |
| 92. | Various professions | 97 |
| 93. | Occupations. Social status | 98 |

**Education** 100

| | | |
|---|---|---|
| 94. | School | 100 |
| 95. | College. University | 101 |
| 96. | Sciences. Disciplines | 102 |
| 97. | Writing system. Orthography | 102 |
| 98. | Foreign languages | 104 |

**Rest. Entertainment. Travel** 106

| | | |
|---|---|---|
| 99. | Trip. Travel | 106 |
| 100. | Hotel | 107 |

**TECHNICAL EQUIPMENT. TRANSPORTATION** 108
**Technical equipment** 108

| | | |
|---|---|---|
| 101. | Computer | 108 |
| 102. | Internet. E-mail | 109 |
| 103. | Electricity | 110 |
| 104. | Tools | 111 |

**Transportation** 114

| | | |
|---|---|---|
| 105. | Airplane | 114 |
| 106. | Train | 115 |
| 107. | Ship | 116 |
| 108. | Airport | 118 |

**Life events** 119

| | | |
|---|---|---|
| 109. | Holidays. Event | 119 |
| 110. | Funerals. Burial | 120 |
| 111. | War. Soldiers | 121 |
| 112. | War. Military actions. Part 1 | 122 |
| 113. | War. Military actions. Part 2 | 123 |
| 114. | Weapons | 125 |
| 115. | Ancient people | 126 |
| 116. | Middle Ages | 127 |
| 117. | Leader. Chief. Authorities | 129 |
| 118. | Breaking the law. Criminals. Part 1 | 129 |
| 119. | Breaking the law. Criminals. Part 2 | 131 |

120. Police. Law. Part 1                                    132
121. Police. Law. Part 2                                    133


**NATURE**                                                  135
**The Earth. Part 1**                                       135

122. Outer space                                            135
123. The Earth                                              136
124. Cardinal directions                                    137
125. Sea. Ocean                                             137
126. Seas' and Oceans' names                                138
127. Mountains                                              139
128. Mountains names                                        140
129. Rivers                                                 141
130. Rivers' names                                          141
131. Forest                                                 142
132. Natural resources                                      143


**The Earth. Part 2**                                       145

133. Weather                                                145
134. Severe weather. Natural disasters                      146


**Fauna**                                                   147

135. Mammals. Predators                                     147
136. Wild animals                                           147
137. Domestic animals                                       149
138. Birds                                                  150
139. Fish. Marine animals                                   151
140. Amphibians. Reptiles                                   152
141. Insects                                                152


**Flora**                                                   154

142. Trees                                                  154
143. Shrubs                                                 155
144. Fruits. Berries                                        155
145. Flowers. Plants                                        156
146. Cereals, grains                                        157


**COUNTRIES. NATIONALITIES**                                158

147. Western Europe                                         158
148. Central and Eastern Europe                             158
149. Former USSR countries                                  159

| | | |
|---|---|---|
| 150. | Asia | 159 |
| 151. | North America | 160 |
| 152. | Central and South America | 160 |
| 153. | Africa | 161 |
| 154. | Australia. Oceania | 161 |
| 155. | Cities | 161 |

# PRONUNCIATION GUIDE

| T&P phonetic alphabet | Persian example | English example |
|---|---|---|
| ['] (ayn) | دعوا [da'vā] | voiced pharyngeal fricative |
| ['] (hamza) | تایید [ta'id ] | glottal stop |
| [a] | رود [ravad] | shorter than in ask |
| [ā] | آتش [ātaš] | calf, palm |
| [b] | بانک [bānk] | baby, book |
| [č] | چند [čand ] | church, French |
| [d] | هشتاد [haštād] | day, doctor |
| [e] | عشق [ešq] | elm, medal |
| [f] | فندک [fandak] | face, food |
| [g] | لوگو [logo] | game, gold |
| [h] | گیاه [giyāh] | home, have |
| [i] | جزیره [jazire] | shorter than in feet |
| [j] | جشن [jašn] | joke, general |
| [k] | کاج [kāj] | clock, kiss |
| [l] | لیمو [limu] | lace, people |
| [m] | ماجرا [mājarā] | magic, milk |
| [n] | نروژ [norvež] | sang, thing |
| [o] | گلف [golf] | pod, John |
| [p] | اپرا [operā] | pencil, private |
| [q] | لاغر [lāqar] | between [g] and [h] |
| [r] | رقم [raqam] | rice, radio |
| [s] | سوپ [sup] | city, boss |
| [š] | دوش [duš] | machine, shark |
| [t] | ترجمه [tarjome] | tourist, trip |
| [u] | نیرو [niru] | book |
| [v] | ورشو [varšow] | very, river |
| [w] | روشن [rowšan] | vase, winter |
| [x] | کاخ [kāx] | as in Scots 'loch' |
| [y] | بیابان [biyābān] | yes, New York |
| [z] | زنجیر [zanjir] | zebra, please |
| [ž] | ژوئن [žuan] | forge, pleasure |

# ABBREVIATIONS
## used in the vocabulary

## English abbreviations

| | | |
|---|---|---|
| **ab.** | - | about |
| **adj** | - | adjective |
| **adv** | - | adverb |
| **anim.** | - | animate |
| **as adj** | - | attributive noun used as adjective |
| **e.g.** | - | for example |
| **etc.** | - | et cetera |
| **fam.** | - | familiar |
| **fem.** | - | feminine |
| **form.** | - | formal |
| **inanim.** | - | inanimate |
| **masc.** | - | masculine |
| **math** | - | mathematics |
| **mil.** | - | military |
| **n** | - | noun |
| **pl** | - | plural |
| **pron.** | - | pronoun |
| **sb** | - | somebody |
| **sing.** | - | singular |
| **sth** | - | something |
| **v aux** | - | auxiliary verb |
| **vi** | - | intransitive verb |
| **vi, vt** | - | intransitive, transitive verb |
| **vt** | - | transitive verb |

# BASIC CONCEPTS

## Basic concepts. Part 1

### 1. Pronouns

| | | |
|---|---|---|
| I, me | man | من |
| you | to | تو |
| | | |
| he, she, it | u | او |
| we | mā | ما |
| you (to a group) | šomā | شما |
| they | ān-hā | آنها |

### 2. Greetings. Salutations. Farewells

| | | |
|---|---|---|
| Hello! (form.) | salām | سلام |
| Good morning! | sobh bexeyr | صبح بخیر |
| Good afternoon! | ruz bexeyr! | روز بخیر! |
| Good evening! | asr bexeyr | عصربخیر |
| | | |
| to say hello | salām kardan | سلام کردن |
| Hi! (hello) | salām | سلام |
| greeting (n) | salām | سلام |
| to greet (vt) | salām kardan | سلام کردن |
| How are you? (form.) | haletān četowr ast? | حالتان چطور است؟ |
| How are you? (fam.) | četorid? | چطورید؟ |
| What's new? | če xabar? | چه خبر؟ |
| | | |
| Goodbye! | xodāhāfez | خداحافظ |
| Bye! | bāy bāy | بای بای |
| See you soon! | be omid-e didār! | به امید دیدار! |
| Farewell! | xodāhāfez! | خداحافظ! |
| to say goodbye | xodāhāfezi kardan | خداحافظی کردن |
| So long! | tā bezudi! | تا بزودی! |
| | | |
| Thank you! | motešakker-am! | متشکرم! |
| Thank you very much! | besyār motešakker-am! | بسیار متشکرم! |
| You're welcome | xāheš mikonam | خواهش می کنم |
| Don't mention it! | tašakkor lāzem nist | تشکر لازم نیست |
| It was nothing | qābel-i nadārad | قابلی ندارد |
| Excuse me! (fam.) | bebaxšid! | ببخشید! |
| to excuse (forgive) | baxšidan | بخشیدن |

15

| to apologize (vi) | ozr xāstan | عذر خواستن |
| My apologies | ozr mixāham | عذرمی خواهم |
| I'm sorry! | bebaxšid! | ببخشید! |
| to forgive (vt) | baxšidan | بخشیدن |
| It's okay! (that's all right) | mohem nist | مهم نیست |
| please (adv) | lotfan | لطفأ |

| Don't forget! | farāmuš nakonid! | فراموش نکنید! |
| Certainly! | albate! | البته! |
| Of course not! | albate ke neh! | البته که نه! |
| Okay! (I agree) | besyār xob! | بسیارخوب! |
| That's enough! | bas ast! | بس است! |

## 3. How to address

| Excuse me, ... | bebaxšid! | ببخشید! |
| mister, sir | āqā | آقا |
| ma'am | xānom | خانم |
| miss | xānom | خانم |
| young man | mard-e javān | مرد جوان |
| young man (little boy, kid) | pesar bače | پسر بچه |
| miss (little girl) | doxtar bačče | دختربچه |

## 4. Cardinal numbers. Part 1

| 0 zero | sefr | صفر |
| 1 one | yek | یک |
| 2 two | do | دو |
| 3 three | se | سه |
| 4 four | čāhār | چهار |

| 5 five | panj | پنج |
| 6 six | šeš | شش |
| 7 seven | haft | هفت |
| 8 eight | hašt | هشت |
| 9 nine | neh | نه |

| 10 ten | dah | ده |
| 11 eleven | yāzdah | یازده |
| 12 twelve | davāzdah | دوازده |
| 13 thirteen | sizdah | سیزده |
| 14 fourteen | čāhārdah | چهارده |

| 15 fifteen | pānzdah | پانزده |
| 16 sixteen | šānzdah | شانزده |
| 17 seventeen | hefdah | هفده |
| 18 eighteen | hijdah | هیجده |
| 19 nineteen | nuzdah | نوزده |

| 20 twenty | bist | بیست |
| 21 twenty-one | bist-o yek | بیست ویک |
| 22 twenty-two | bist-o do | بیست ودو |
| 23 twenty-three | bist-o se | بیست وسه |

| 30 thirty | si | سی |
| 31 thirty-one | si-yo yek | سی ویک |
| 32 thirty-two | si-yo do | سی ودو |
| 33 thirty-three | si-yo se | سی وسه |

| 40 forty | čehel | چهل |
| 41 forty-one | čehel-o yek | چهل ویک |
| 42 forty-two | čehel-o do | چهل ودو |
| 43 forty-three | čehel-o se | چهل وسه |

| 50 fifty | panjāh | پنجاه |
| 51 fifty-one | panjāh-o yek | پنجاه ویک |
| 52 fifty-two | panjāh-o do | پنجاه ودو |
| 53 fifty-three | panjāh-o se | پنجاه وسه |

| 60 sixty | šast | شصت |
| 61 sixty-one | šast-o yek | شصت ویک |
| 62 sixty-two | šast-o do | شصت ودو |
| 63 sixty-three | šast-o se | شصت وسه |

| 70 seventy | haftād | هفتاد |
| 71 seventy-one | haftād-o yek | هفتاد ویک |
| 72 seventy-two | haftād-o do | هفتاد ودو |
| 73 seventy-three | haftād-o se | هفتاد وسه |

| 80 eighty | haštād | هشتاد |
| 81 eighty-one | haštād-o yek | هشتاد ویک |
| 82 eighty-two | haštād-o do | هشتاد ودو |
| 83 eighty-three | haštād-o se | هشتاد وسه |

| 90 ninety | navad | نود |
| 91 ninety-one | navad-o yek | نود ویک |
| 92 ninety-two | navad-o do | نود ودو |
| 93 ninety-three | navad-o se | نود وسه |

## 5. Cardinal numbers. Part 2

| 100 one hundred | sad | صد |
| 200 two hundred | devist | دویست |
| 300 three hundred | sisad | سیصد |
| 400 four hundred | čāhārsad | چهارصد |
| 500 five hundred | pānsad | پانصد |

| 600 six hundred | šeššad | ششصد |
| 700 seven hundred | haftsad | هفتصد |

| | | |
|---|---|---|
| 800 eight hundred | haštsad | هشتصد |
| 900 nine hundred | nohsad | نهصد |
| | | |
| 1000 one thousand | hezār | هزار |
| 2000 two thousand | dohezār | دوهزار |
| 3000 three thousand | se hezār | سه هزار |
| 10000 ten thousand | dah hezār | ده هزار |
| one hundred thousand | sad hezār | صد هزار |
| million | milyun | میلیون |
| billion | milyārd | میلیارد |

## 6. Ordinal numbers

| | | |
|---|---|---|
| first (adj) | avvalin | اولین |
| second (adj) | dovvomin | دومین |
| third (adj) | sevvomin | سومین |
| fourth (adj) | čāhāromin | چهارمین |
| fifth (adj) | panjomin | پنجمین |
| | | |
| sixth (adj) | šešomin | ششمین |
| seventh (adj) | haftomin | هفتمین |
| eighth (adj) | haštomin | هشتمین |
| ninth (adj) | nohomin | نهمین |
| tenth (adj) | dahomin | دهمین |

## 7. Numbers. Fractions

| | | |
|---|---|---|
| fraction | kasr | کسر |
| one half | yek dovvom | یک دوم |
| one third | yek sevvom | یک سوم |
| one quarter | yek čāhārom | یک چهارم |
| | | |
| one eighth | yek panjom | یک هشتم |
| one tenth | yek dahom | یک دهم |
| two thirds | do sevvom | دو سوم |
| three quarters | se čāhārrom | سه چهارم |

## 8. Numbers. Basic operations

| | | |
|---|---|---|
| subtraction | tafriq | تفریق |
| to subtract (vi, vt) | tafriq kardan | تفریق کردن |
| division | taqsim | تقسیم |
| to divide (vt) | taqsim kardan | تقسیم کردن |
| | | |
| addition | jam' | جمع |
| to add up (vt) | jam' kardan | جمع کردن |

| to add (vi, vt) | ezāfe kardan | اضافه کردن |
| multiplication | zarb | ضرب |
| to multiply (vt) | zarb kardan | ضرب کردن |

## 9. Numbers. Miscellaneous

| digit, figure | raqam | رقم |
| number | adad | عدد |
| numeral | adadi | عددی |
| minus sign | manfi | منفی |
| plus sign | mosbat | مثبت |
| formula | formul | فرمول |

| calculation | mohāsebe | محاسبه |
| to count (vi, vt) | šemordan | شمردن |
| to count up | mohāsebe kardan | محاسبه کردن |
| to compare (vt) | moqāyse kardan | مقایسه کردن |

| How much? | čeqadr? | چقدر؟ |
| sum, total | jam'-e kol | جمع کل |
| result | natije | نتیجه |
| remainder | bāqimānde | باقیمانده |

| a few (e.g., ~ years ago) | čand | چند |
| little (I had ~ time) | kami | کمی |
| the rest | baqiye | بقیه |
| one and a half | yek-o nim | یک و نیم |
| dozen | dojin | دوجین |

| in half (adv) | be do qesmat | به دو قسمت |
| equally (evenly) | be tāsavi | به تساوی |
| half | nim | نیم |
| time (three ~s) | daf'e | دفعه |

## 10. The most important verbs. Part 1

| to advise (vt) | nasihat kardan | نصیحت کردن |
| to agree (say yes) | movāfeqat kardan | موافقت کردن |
| to answer (vi, vt) | javāb dādan | جواب دادن |
| to apologize (vi) | ozr xāstan | عذر خواستن |
| to arrive (vi) | residan | رسیدن |

| to ask (~ oneself) | porsidan | پرسیدن |
| to ask (~ sb to do sth) | xāstan | خواستن |
| to be (vi) | budan | بودن |

| to be afraid | tarsidan | ترسیدن |
| to be hungry | gorosne budan | گرسنه بودن |

| to be interested in ... | alāqe dāštan | علاقه داشتن |
| to be needed | hāmi budan | حامی بودن |
| to be surprised | mote'ajjeb šodan | متعجب شدن |

| to be thirsty | tešne budan | تشنه بودن |
| to begin (vt) | šoru' kardan | شروع کردن |
| to belong to ... | ta'alloq dāštan | تعلق داشتن |
| to boast (vi) | be rox kešidan | به رخ کشیدن |
| to break (split into pieces) | šekastan | شکستن |

| to call (~ for help) | komak xāstan | کمک خواستن |
| can (v aux) | tavānestan | توانستن |
| to catch (vt) | gereftan | گرفتن |
| to change (vt) | avaz kardan | عوض کردن |
| to choose (select) | entexāb kardan | انتخاب کردن |

| to come down (the stairs) | pāyin āmadan | پایین آمدن |
| to compare (vt) | moqāyse kardan | مقایسه کردن |
| to complain (vi, vt) | šekāyat kardan | شکایت کردن |
| to confuse (mix up) | qāti kardan | قاطی کردن |
| to continue (vt) | edāme dādan | ادامه دادن |
| to control (vt) | kontorol kardan | کنترل کردن |

| to cook (dinner) | poxtan | پختن |
| to cost (vt) | qeymat dāštan | قیمت داشتن |
| to count (add up) | šemordan | شمردن |
| to count on ... | hesāb kardan | حساب کردن |
| to create (vt) | ijād kardan | ایجاد کردن |
| to cry (weep) | gerye kardan | گریه کردن |

## 11. The most important verbs. Part 2

| to deceive (vi, vt) | farib dādan | فریب دادن |
| to decorate (tree, street) | tazyin kardan | تزیین کردن |
| to defend (a country, etc.) | defā' kardan | دفاع کردن |
| to demand (request firmly) | darxāst kardan | درخواست کردن |
| to dig (vt) | kandan | کندن |

| to discuss (vt) | bahs kardan | بحث کردن |
| to do (vt) | anjām dādan | انجام دادن |
| to doubt (have doubts) | šok dāštan | شک داشتن |
| to drop (let fall) | andāxtan | انداختن |
| to enter (room, house, etc.) | vāred šodan | وارد شدن |

| to excuse (forgive) | baxšidan | بخشیدن |
| to exist (vi) | vojud dāštan | وجود داشتن |
| to expect (foresee) | pišbini kardan | پیش بینی کردن |
| to explain (vt) | touzih dādan | توضیح دادن |
| to fall (vi) | oftādan | افتادن |

| to find (vt) | peydā kardan | پیدا کردن |
| to finish (vt) | be pāyān resāndan | به پایان رساندن |
| to fly (vi) | parvāz kardan | پرواز کردن |
| to follow ... (come after) | donbāl kardan | دنبال کردن |
| to forget (vi, vt) | farāmuš kardan | فراموش کردن |
| | | |
| to forgive (vt) | baxšidan | بخشیدن |
| to give (vt) | dādan | دادن |
| to give a hint | sarnax dādan | سرنخ دادن |
| to go (on foot) | raftan | رفتن |
| | | |
| to go for a swim | ābtani kardan | آبتنی کردن |
| to go out (for dinner, etc.) | birun raftan | بیرون رفتن |
| to guess (the answer) | hads zadan | حدس زدن |
| | | |
| to have (vt) | dāštan | داشتن |
| to have breakfast | sobhāne xordan | صبحانه خوردن |
| to have dinner | šām xordan | شام خوردن |
| to have lunch | nāhār xordan | ناهار خوردن |
| to hear (vt) | šenidan | شنیدن |
| | | |
| to help (vt) | komak kardan | کمک کردن |
| to hide (vt) | penhān kardan | پنهان کردن |
| to hope (vi, vt) | omid dāštan | امید داشتن |
| to hunt (vi, vt) | šekār kardan | شکار کردن |
| to hurry (vi) | ajale kardan | عجله کردن |

## 12. The most important verbs. Part 3

| to inform (vt) | āgah kardan | آگاه کردن |
| to insist (vi, vt) | esrār kardan | اصرار کردن |
| to insult (vt) | towhin kardan | توهین کردن |
| to invite (vt) | da'vat kardan | دعوت کردن |
| to joke (vi) | šuxi kardan | شوخی کردن |
| | | |
| to keep (vt) | hefz kardan | حفظ کردن |
| to keep silent | sāket māndan | ساکت ماندن |
| to kill (vt) | koštan | کشتن |
| to know (sb) | šenāxtan | شناختن |
| to know (sth) | dānestan | دانستن |
| to laugh (vi) | xandidan | خندیدن |
| | | |
| to liberate (city, etc.) | āzād kardan | آزاد کردن |
| to like (I like ...) | dust dāštan | دوست داشتن |
| to look for ... (search) | jostoju kardan | جستجو کردن |
| to love (sb) | dust dāštan | دوست داشتن |
| to make a mistake | eštebāh kardan | اشتباه کردن |
| | | |
| to manage, to run | edāre kardan | اداره کردن |
| to mean (signify) | ma'ni dāštan | معنی داشتن |

| to mention (talk about) | zekr kardan | ذکر کردن |
| to miss (school, etc.) | qāyeb budan | غایب بودن |
| to notice (see) | motevajjeh šodan | متوجه شدن |

| to object (vi, vt) | moxalefat kardan | مخالفت کردن |
| to observe (see) | mošāhede kardan | مشاهده کردن |
| to open (vt) | bāz kardan | باز کردن |
| to order (meal, etc.) | sefāreš dādan | سفارش دادن |
| to order (mil.) | farmān dādan | فرمان دادن |
| to own (possess) | sāheb budan | صاحب بودن |

| to participate (vi) | šerekat kardan | شرکت کردن |
| to pay (vi, vt) | pardāxtan | پرداختن |
| to permit (vt) | ejāze dādan | اجازه دادن |
| to plan (vt) | barnāmerizi kardan | برنامه ریزی کردن |
| to play (children) | bāzi kardan | بازی کردن |

| to pray (vi, vt) | do'ā kardan | دعا کردن |
| to prefer (vt) | tarjih dādan | ترجیح دادن |
| to promise (vt) | qowl dādan | قول دادن |
| to pronounce (vt) | talaffoz kardan | تلفظ کردن |
| to propose (vt) | pišnahād dādan | پیشنهاد دادن |
| to punish (vt) | tanbih kardan | تنبیه کردن |

## 13. The most important verbs. Part 4

| to read (vi, vt) | xāndan | خواندن |
| to recommend (vt) | towsie kardan | توصیه کردن |
| to refuse (vi, vt) | rad kardan | رد کردن |
| to regret (be sorry) | afsus xordan | افسوس خوردن |
| to rent (sth from sb) | ejāre kardan | اجاره کردن |

| to repeat (say again) | tekrār kardan | تکرار کردن |
| to reserve, to book | rezerv kardan | رزرو کردن |
| to run (vi) | davidan | دویدن |
| to save (rescue) | najāt dādan | نجات دادن |
| to say (~ thank you) | goftan | گفتن |

| to scold (vt) | da'vā kardan | دعوا کردن |
| to see (vt) | didan | دیدن |
| to sell (vt) | foruxtan | فروختن |
| to send (vt) | ferestādan | فرستادن |
| to shoot (vi) | tirandāzi kardan | تیراندازی کردن |

| to shout (vi) | faryād zadan | فریاد زدن |
| to show (vt) | nešān dādan | نشان دادن |
| to sign (document) | emzā kardan | امضا کردن |
| to sit down (vi) | nešastan | نشستن |
| to smile (vi) | labxand zadan | لبخند زدن |
| to speak (vi, vt) | harf zadan | حرف زدن |

| | | |
|---|---|---|
| to steal (money, etc.) | dozdidan | دزدیدن |
| to stop (for pause, etc.) | motevaghef šhodan | متوقف شدن |
| to stop (please ~ calling me) | bas kardan | بس کردن |

| | | |
|---|---|---|
| to study (vt) | dars xāndan | درس خواندن |
| to swim (vi) | šenā kardan | شنا کردن |
| to take (vt) | bardāštan | برداشتن |
| to think (vi, vt) | fekr kardan | فکر کردن |
| to threaten (vt) | tahdid kardan | تهدید کردن |

| | | |
|---|---|---|
| to touch (with hands) | lams kardan | لمس کردن |
| to translate (vt) | tarjome kardan | ترجمه کردن |
| to trust (vt) | etminān kardan | اطمینان کردن |
| to try (attempt) | talāš kardan | تلاش کردن |
| to turn (e.g., ~ left) | pičidan | پیچیدن |

| | | |
|---|---|---|
| to underestimate (vt) | dast-e kam gereftan | دست کم گرفتن |
| to understand (vt) | fahmidan | فهمیدن |
| to unite (vt) | mottahed kardan | متحد کردن |
| to wait (vt) | montazer budan | منتظر بودن |

| | | |
|---|---|---|
| to want (wish, desire) | xāstan | خواستن |
| to warn (vt) | hošdār dādan | هشدار دادن |
| to work (vi) | kār kardan | کار کردن |
| to write (vt) | neveštan | نوشتن |
| to write down | neveštan | نوشتن |

## 14. Colors

| | | |
|---|---|---|
| color | rang | رنگ |
| shade (tint) | teyf-e rang | طیف رنگ |
| hue | rangmaye | رنگمایه |
| rainbow | rangin kamān | رنگین کمان |

| | | |
|---|---|---|
| white (adj) | sefid | سفید |
| black (adj) | siyāh | سیاه |
| gray (adj) | xākestari | خاکستری |

| | | |
|---|---|---|
| green (adj) | sabz | سبز |
| yellow (adj) | zard | زرد |
| red (adj) | sorx | سرخ |

| | | |
|---|---|---|
| blue (adj) | abi | آبی |
| light blue (adj) | ābi rowšan | آبی روشن |
| pink (adj) | surati | صورتی |
| orange (adj) | nārenji | نارنجی |
| violet (adj) | banafš | بنفش |
| brown (adj) | qahve i | قهوه ای |
| golden (adj) | talāyi | طلایی |

| silvery (adj) | noqre i | نقره ای |
| beige (adj) | baž | بژ |
| cream (adj) | kerem | کرم |
| turquoise (adj) | firuze i | فیروزه ای |
| cherry red (adj) | ālbāluyi | آلبالویی |
| lilac (adj) | banafš yasi | بنفش یاسی |
| crimson (adj) | zereški | زرشکی |

| light (adj) | rowšan | روشن |
| dark (adj) | tire | تیره |
| bright, vivid (adj) | rowšan | روشن |

| colored (pencils) | rangi | رنگی |
| color (e.g., ~ film) | rangi | رنگی |
| black-and-white (adj) | siyāh-o sefid | سیاه و سفید |
| plain (one-colored) | yek rang | یک رنگ |
| multicolored (adj) | rangārang | رنگارنگ |

## 15. Questions

| Who? | če kas-i? | چه کسی؟ |
| What? | če čiz-i? | چه چیزی؟ |
| Where? (at, in) | kojā? | کجا؟ |
| Where (to)? | kojā? | کجا؟ |
| From where? | az kojā? | از کجا؟ |
| When? | če vaqt? | چه وقت؟ |
| Why? (What for?) | čerā? | چرا؟ |
| Why? (~ are you crying?) | čerā? | چرا؟ |

| What for? | barā-ye če? | برای چه؟ |
| How? (in what way) | četor? | چطور؟ |
| What? (What kind of ...?) | kodām? | کدام؟ |
| Which? | kodām? | کدام؟ |

| To whom? | barā-ye ki? | برای کی؟ |
| About whom? | dar bāre-ye ki? | درباره کی؟ |
| About what? | darbāre-ye či? | درباره چی؟ |
| With whom? | bā ki? | با کی؟ |

| How many? How much? | čeqadr? | چقدر؟ |
| Whose? | māl-e ki? | مال کی؟ |

## 16. Prepositions

| with (accompanied by) | bā | با |
| without | bedune | بدون |
| to (indicating direction) | be | به |
| about (talking ~ ...) | rāje' be | راجع به |

| before (in time) | piš az | پیش از |
| in front of … | dar moqābel | در مقابل |

| under (beneath, below) | zir | زیر |
| above (over) | bālā-ye | بالای |
| on (atop) | ruy | روی |
| from (off, out of) | az | از |
| of (made from) | az | از |

| in (e.g., ~ ten minutes) | tā | تا |
| over (across the top of) | az bālāye | از بالای |

## 17. Function words. Adverbs. Part 1

| Where? (at, in) | kojā? | کجا؟ |
| here (adv) | in jā | این جا |
| there (adv) | ānjā | آنجا |

| somewhere (to be) | jā-yi | جایی |
| nowhere (not anywhere) | hič kojā | هیچ کجا |

| by (near, beside) | nazdik | نزدیک |
| by the window | nazdik panjere | نزدیک پنجره |

| Where (to)? | kojā? | کجا؟ |
| here (e.g., come ~!) | in jā | این جا |
| there (e.g., to go ~) | ānjā | آنجا |
| from here (adv) | az injā | از اینجا |
| from there (adv) | az ānjā | از آنجا |

| close (adv) | nazdik | نزدیک |
| far (adv) | dur | دور |

| near (e.g., ~ Paris) | nazdik | نزدیک |
| nearby (adv) | nazdik | نزدیک |
| not far (adv) | nazdik | نزدیک |

| left (adj) | čap | چپ |
| on the left | dast-e čap | دست چپ |
| to the left | be čap | به چپ |

| right (adj) | rāst | راست |
| on the right | dast-e rāst | دست راست |
| to the right | be rāst | به راست |

| in front (adv) | jelo | جلو |
| front (as adj) | jelo | جلو |
| ahead (the kids ran ~) | jelo | جلو |
| behind (adv) | aqab | عقب |
| from behind | az aqab | از عقب |

| back (towards the rear) | aqab | عقب |
| middle | vasat | وسط |
| in the middle | dar vasat | در وسط |

| at the side | pahlu | پهلو |
| everywhere (adv) | hame jā | همه جا |
| around (in all directions) | atrāf | اطراف |

| from inside | az daxel | از داخل |
| somewhere (to go) | jā-yi | جایی |
| straight (directly) | mostaqim | مستقیم |
| back (e.g., come ~) | aqab | عقب |

| from anywhere | az har jā | از هر جا |
| from somewhere | az yek jā-yi | از یک جایی |

| firstly (adv) | avvalan | اولاً |
| secondly (adv) | dumā | دوما |
| thirdly (adv) | sālesan | ثالثاً |

| suddenly (adv) | nāgahān | ناگهان |
| at first (in the beginning) | dar avval | در اول |
| for the first time | barā-ye avvalin bār | برای اولین بار |
| long before ... | xeyli vaqt piš | خیلی وقت پیش |
| anew (over again) | az now | از نو |
| for good (adv) | barā-ye hamiše | برای همیشه |

| never (adv) | hič vaqt | هیچ وقت |
| again (adv) | dobāre | دوباره |
| now (adv) | alān | الان |
| often (adv) | aqlab | اغلب |
| then (adv) | ān vaqt | آن وقت |
| urgently (quickly) | foran | فوراً |
| usually (adv) | ma'mulan | معمولاً |

| by the way, ... | rāst-i | راستی |
| possible (that is ~) | momken ast | ممکن است |
| probably (adv) | ehtemālan | احتمالاً |
| maybe (adv) | šāyad | شاید |
| besides ... | bealāve | بعلاوه |
| that's why ... | be hamin xāter | به همین خاطر |
| in spite of ... | alāraqm | علیرغم |
| thanks to ... | be lotf | به لطف |

| what (pron.) | če? | چه؟ |
| that (conj.) | ke | که |
| something | yek čiz-i | یک چیزی |
| anything (something) | yek kāri | یک کاری |
| nothing | hič čiz | هیچ چیز |

| who (pron.) | ki | کی |
| someone | yek kas-i | یک کسی |

| somebody | yek kas-i | یک کسی |
| nobody | hič kas | هیچ کس |
| nowhere (a voyage to ~) | hič kojā | هیچ کجا |
| nobody's | māl-e hičkas | مال هیچ کس |
| somebody's | har kas-i | هر کسی |

| so (I'm ~ glad) | xeyli | خیلی |
| also (as well) | ham | هم |
| too (as well) | ham | هم |

## 18. Function words. Adverbs. Part 2

| Why? | čerā? | چرا؟ |
| for some reason | be dalil-i | به دلیلی |
| because ... | čon | چون |
| for some purpose | barā-ye maqsudi | برای مقصودی |

| and | va | و |
| or | yā | یا |
| but | ammā | اما |
| for (e.g., ~ me) | barā-ye | برای |

| too (~ many people) | besyār | بسیار |
| only (exclusively) | faqat | فقط |
| exactly (adv) | daqiqan | دقیقا |
| about (more or less) | taqriban | تقریباً |

| approximately (adv) | taqriban | تقریباً |
| approximate (adj) | taqribi | تقریبی |
| almost (adv) | taqriban | تقریباً |
| the rest | baqiye | بقیه |

| the other (second) | digar | دیگر |
| other (different) | digar | دیگر |
| each (adj) | har | هر |
| any (no matter which) | har | هر |
| many, much (a lot of) | ziyād | زیاد |
| many people | besyāri | بسیاری |
| all (everyone) | hame | همه |

| in return for ... | dar avaz | در عوض |
| in exchange (adv) | dar barābar | در برابر |
| by hand (made) | dasti | دستی |
| hardly (negative opinion) | baid ast | بعید است |

| probably (adv) | ehtemālan | احتمالاً |
| on purpose (intentionally) | amdan | عمداً |
| by accident (adv) | tasādofi | تصادفی |
| very (adv) | besyār | بسیار |
| for example (adv) | masalan | مثلاً |

| | | |
|---|---|---|
| between | beyn | بین |
| among | miyān | میان |
| so much (such a lot) | in qadr | این قدر |
| especially (adv) | maxsusan | مخصوصاً |

# Basic concepts. Part 2

## 19. Weekdays

| Monday | došanbe | دوشنبه |
| Tuesday | se šanbe | سه شنبه |
| Wednesday | čāhāršanbe | چهارشنبه |
| Thursday | panj šanbe | پنج شنبه |
| Friday | jom'e | جمعه |
| Saturday | šanbe | شنبه |
| Sunday | yek šanbe | یک شنبه |

| today (adv) | emruz | امروز |
| tomorrow (adv) | fardā | فردا |
| the day after tomorrow | pas fardā | پس فردا |
| yesterday (adv) | diruz | دیروز |
| the day before yesterday | pariruz | پریروز |

| day | ruz | روز |
| working day | ruz-e kāri | روز کاری |
| public holiday | ruz-e jašn | روز جشن |
| day off | ruz-e ta'til | روز تعطیل |
| weekend | āxar-e hafte | آخر هفته |

| all day long | tamām-e ruz | تمام روز |
| the next day (adv) | ruz-e ba'd | روز بعد |
| two days ago | do ruz-e piš | دو روز پیش |
| the day before | ruz-e qabl | روز قبل |
| daily (adj) | ruzāne | روزانه |
| every day (adv) | har ruz | هر روز |

| week | hafte | هفته |
| last week (adv) | hafte-ye gozašte | هفته گذشته |
| next week (adv) | hafte-ye āyande | هفته آینده |
| weekly (adj) | haftegi | هفتگی |
| every week (adv) | har hafte | هر هفته |
| twice a week | do bār dar hafte | دو بار درهفته |
| every Tuesday | har sešanbe | هر سه شنبه |

## 20. Hours. Day and night

| morning | sobh | صبح |
| in the morning | sobh | صبح |
| noon, midday | zohr | ظهر |

| | | |
|---|---|---|
| in the afternoon | ba'd az zohr | بعد ازظهر |
| evening | asr | عصر |
| in the evening | asr | عصر |
| night | šab | شب |
| at night | šab | شب |
| midnight | nesfe šab | نصفه شب |
| | | |
| second | sānie | ثانیه |
| minute | daqiqe | دقیقه |
| hour | sā'at | ساعت |
| half an hour | nim sā'at | نیم ساعت |
| a quarter-hour | yek rob' | یک ربع |
| fifteen minutes | pānzdah daqiqe | پانزده دقیقه |
| 24 hours | šabāne ruz | شبانه روز |
| | | |
| sunrise | tolu-'e āftāb | طلوع آفتاب |
| dawn | sahar | سحر |
| early morning | sobh-e zud | صبح زود |
| sunset | qorub | غروب |
| | | |
| early in the morning | sobh-e zud | صبح زود |
| this morning | emruz sobh | امروز صبح |
| tomorrow morning | fardā sobh | فردا صبح |
| | | |
| this afternoon | emruz zohr | امروز ظهر |
| in the afternoon | ba'd az zohr | بعد ازظهر |
| tomorrow afternoon | fardā ba'd az zohr | فردا بعد ازظهر |
| | | |
| tonight (this evening) | emšab | امشب |
| tomorrow night | fardā šab | فردا شب |
| | | |
| at 3 o'clock sharp | sar-e sā'at-e se | سر ساعت ۳ |
| about 4 o'clock | nazdik-e sā'at-e čāhār | نزدیک ساعت ۴ |
| by 12 o'clock | nazdik zohr | نزدیک ظهر |
| | | |
| in 20 minutes | bist daqiqe-ye digar | ۲۰ دقیقه دیگر |
| in an hour | yek sā'at-e digar | یک ساعت دیگر |
| on time (adv) | be moqe' | به موقع |
| | | |
| a quarter of ... | yek rob' be | یک ربع به |
| within an hour | yek sā'at-e digar | یک ساعت دیگر |
| every 15 minutes | har pānzdah daqiqe | هر ۵۱ دقیقه |
| round the clock | šabāne ruz | شبانه روز |

## 21. Months. Seasons

| | | |
|---|---|---|
| January | žānvie | ژانویه |
| February | fevriye | فوریه |
| March | mārs | مارس |
| April | āvril | آوریل |

| May | meh | مه |
| June | žuan | ژوئن |

| July | žuiye | ژوئیه |
| August | owt | اوت |
| September | septāmbr | سپتامبر |
| October | oktobr | اکتبر |
| November | novāmbr | نوامبر |
| December | desāmr | دسامبر |

| spring | bahār | بهار |
| in spring | dar bahār | در بهار |
| spring (as adj) | bahāri | بهاری |

| summer | tābestān | تابستان |
| in summer | dar tābestān | در تابستان |
| summer (as adj) | tābestāni | تابستانی |

| fall | pāyiz | پاییز |
| in fall | dar pāyiz | در پاییز |
| fall (as adj) | pāyizi | پاییزی |

| winter | zemestān | زمستان |
| in winter | dar zemestān | در زمستان |
| winter (as adj) | zemestāni | زمستانی |

| month | māh | ماه |
| this month | in māh | این ماه |
| next month | māh-e āyande | ماه آینده |
| last month | māh-e gozašte | ماه گذشته |

| a month ago | yek māh qabl | یک ماه قبل |
| in a month (a month later) | yek māh digar | یک ماه دیگر |
| in 2 months (2 months later) | do māh-e digar | ۲ماه دیگر |
| the whole month | tamām-e māh | تمام ماه |
| all month long | tamām-e māh | تمام ماه |

| monthly (~ magazine) | māhāne | ماهانه |
| monthly (adv) | māhāne | ماهانه |
| every month | har māh | هر ماه |
| twice a month | do bār dar māh | دو بار درماه |

| year | sāl | سال |
| this year | emsāl | امسال |
| next year | sāl-e āyande | سال آینده |
| last year | sāl-e gozašte | سال گذشته |

| a year ago | yek sāl qabl | یک سال قبل |
| in a year | yek sāl-e digar | یک سال دیگر |
| in two years | do sāl-e digar | ۲سال دیگر |
| the whole year | tamām-e sāl | تمام سال |

| all year long | tamām-e sāl | تمام سال |
| every year | har sāl | هر سال |
| annual (adj) | sālāne | سالانه |
| annually (adv) | sālāne | سالانه |
| 4 times a year | čāhār bār dar sāl | چهار بار در سال |

| date (e.g., today's ~) | tārix | تاریخ |
| date (e.g., ~ of birth) | tārix | تاریخ |
| calendar | taqvim | تقویم |

| half a year | nim sāl | نیم سال |
| six months | nim sāl | نیم سال |
| season (summer, etc.) | fasl | فصل |
| century | qarn | قرن |

## 22. Units of measurement

| weight | vazn | وزن |
| length | tul | طول |
| width | arz | عرض |
| height | ertefāʿ | ارتفاع |
| depth | omq | عمق |
| volume | hajm | حجم |
| area | masāhat | مساحت |

| gram | garm | گرم |
| milligram | mili geram | میلی گرم |
| kilogram | kilugeram | کیلوگرم |
| ton | ton | تن |
| pound | pond | پوند |
| ounce | ons | اونس |

| meter | metr | متر |
| millimeter | mili metr | میلی متر |
| centimeter | sāntimetr | سانتیمتر |
| kilometer | kilumetr | کیلومتر |
| mile | māyel | مایل |

| inch | inč | اینچ |
| foot | fowt | فوت |
| yard | yārd | یارد |

| square meter | metr morabbaʿ | متر مربع |
| hectare | hektār | هکتار |

| liter | litr | لیتر |
| degree | daraje | درجه |
| volt | volt | ولت |
| ampere | āmper | آمپر |
| horsepower | asb-e boxār | اسب بخار |

| quantity | meqdār | مقدار |
|---|---|---|
| a little bit of ... | kami | کمی |
| half | nim | نیم |
| dozen | dojin | دوجین |
| piece (item) | tā | تا |

| size | andāze | اندازه |
|---|---|---|
| scale (map ~) | meqyās | مقیاس |

| minimal (adj) | haddeaqal | حداقل |
|---|---|---|
| the smallest (adj) | kučaktarin | کوچکترین |
| medium (adj) | motevasset | متوسط |
| maximal (adj) | haddeaksar | حداکثر |
| the largest (adj) | bištarin | بیشترین |

## 23. Containers

| canning jar (glass ~) | šišeh konserv | شیشه کنسرو |
|---|---|---|
| can | quti | قوطی |
| bucket | satl | سطل |
| barrel | boške | بشکه |

| wash basin (e.g., plastic ~) | tašt | تشت |
|---|---|---|
| tank (100L water ~) | maxzan | مخزن |
| hip flask | qomqome | قمقمه |
| jerrycan | dabbe | دبه |
| tank (e.g., tank car) | maxzan | مخزن |

| mug | livān | لیوان |
|---|---|---|
| cup (of coffee, etc.) | fenjān | فنجان |
| saucer | na'lbeki | نعلبکی |
| glass (tumbler) | estekān | استکان |
| wine glass | gilās-e šarāb | گیلاس شراب |
| stock pot (soup pot) | qāblame | قابلمه |

| bottle (~ of wine) | botri | بطری |
|---|---|---|
| neck (of the bottle, etc.) | gardan-e botri | گردن بطری |

| carafe (decanter) | tong | تنگ |
|---|---|---|
| pitcher | pārč | پارچ |
| vessel (container) | zarf | ظرف |
| pot (crock, stoneware ~) | sofāl | سفال |
| vase | goldān | گلدان |

| bottle (perfume ~) | botri | بطری |
|---|---|---|
| vial, small bottle | viyāl | ویال |
| tube (of toothpaste) | tiyub | تیوب |

| sack (bag) | kise | کیسه |
|---|---|---|
| bag (paper ~, plastic ~) | pākat | پاکت |

| pack (of cigarettes, etc.) | baste | بسته |
| box (e.g., shoebox) | ja'be | جعبه |
| crate | sanduq | صندوق |
| basket | sabad | سبد |

# HUMAN BEING

## Human being. The body

### 24. Head

| | | |
|---|---|---|
| head | sar | سر |
| face | surat | صورت |
| nose | bini | بینی |
| mouth | dahān | دهان |
| | | |
| eye | češm | چشم |
| eyes | češm-hā | چشم ها |
| pupil | mardomak | مردمک |
| eyebrow | abru | ابرو |
| eyelash | može | مژه |
| eyelid | pelek | پلک |
| | | |
| tongue | zabān | زبان |
| tooth | dandān | دندان |
| lips | lab-hā | لب ها |
| cheekbones | ostexānhā-ye gune | استخوان های گونه |
| gum | lase | لثه |
| palate | saqf-e dahān | سقف دهان |
| | | |
| nostrils | surāxhā-ye bini | سوراخ های بینی |
| chin | čāne | چانه |
| jaw | fak | فک |
| cheek | gune | گونه |
| | | |
| forehead | pišāni | پیشانی |
| temple | gijgāh | گیجگاه |
| ear | guš | گوش |
| back of the head | pas gardan | پس گردن |
| neck | gardan | گردن |
| throat | galu | گلو |
| | | |
| hair | mu-hā | مو ها |
| hairstyle | model-e mu | مدل مو |
| haircut | model-e mu | مدل مو |
| wig | kolāh-e gis | کلاه گیس |
| | | |
| mustache | sebil | سبیل |
| beard | riš | ریش |
| to have (a beard, etc.) | gozāštan | گذاشتن |

| braid | muy-ye bāfte | موی بافته |
| sideburns | xatt-e riš | خط ریش |

| red-haired (adj) | muqermez | موقرمز |
| gray (hair) | sefid-e mu | سفید مو |
| bald (adj) | tās | طاس |
| bald patch | tāsi | طاسی |

| ponytail | dom-e asbi | دم اسبی |
| bangs | čatri | چتری |

## 25. Human body

| hand | dast | دست |
| arm | bāzu | بازو |

| finger | angošt | انگشت |
| toe | šast-e pā | شصت پا |
| thumb | šost | شست |
| little finger | angošt-e kučak | انگشت کوچک |
| nail | nāxon | ناخن |

| fist | mošt | مشت |
| palm | kaf-e dast | کف دست |
| wrist | moč-e dast | مچ دست |
| forearm | sā'ed | ساعد |
| elbow | āranj | آرنج |
| shoulder | ketf | کتف |

| leg | pā | پا |
| foot | pā | پا |
| knee | zānu | زانو |
| calf (part of leg) | sāq | ساق |
| hip | rān | ران |
| heel | pāšne-ye pā | پاشنۀ پا |

| body | badan | بدن |
| stomach | šekam | شکم |
| chest | sine | سینه |
| breast | sine | سینه |
| flank | pahlu | پهلو |
| back | pošt | پشت |
| lower back | kamar | کمر |
| waist | dur-e kamar | دور کمر |
| navel (belly button) | nāf | ناف |
| buttocks | nešiman-e gāh | نشیمن گاه |
| bottom | bāsan | باسن |
| beauty mark | xāl | خال |
| birthmark (café au lait spot) | xāl-e mādarzād | خال مادرزاد |

| tattoo | xāl kubi | خال کوبی |
| scar | jā-ye zaxm | جای زخم |

# Clothing & Accessories

## 26. Outerwear. Coats

| clothes | lebās | لباس |
| outerwear | lebās-e ru | لباس رو |
| winter clothing | lebās-e zemestāni | لباس زمستانی |

| coat (overcoat) | pāltow | پالتو |
| fur coat | pālto-ye pustin | پالتوی پوستین |
| fur jacket | kot-e pustin | کت پوستین |
| down coat | kāpšan | کاپشن |

| jacket (e.g., leather ~) | kot | کت |
| raincoat (trenchcoat, etc.) | bārāni | بارانی |
| waterproof (adj) | zed-e āb | ضد آب |

## 27. Men's & women's clothing

| shirt (button shirt) | pirāhan | پیراهن |
| pants | šalvār | شلوار |
| jeans | jin | جین |
| suit jacket | kot | کت |
| suit | kat-o šalvār | کت و شلوار |

| dress (frock) | lebās | لباس |
| skirt | dāman | دامن |
| blouse | boluz | بلوز |
| knitted jacket (cardigan, etc.) | jeliqe-ye kešbāf | جلیقه کشباف |
| jacket (of woman's suit) | kot | کت |

| T-shirt | tey šarr-at | تی شرت |
| shorts (short trousers) | šalvarak | شلوارک |
| tracksuit | lebās-e varzeši | لباس ورزشی |
| bathrobe | howle-ye hamām | حوله حمام |
| pajamas | pižāme | پیژامه |

| sweater | poliver | پلیور |
| pullover | poliver | پلیور |

| vest | jeliqe | جلیقه |
| tailcoat | kat-e dāman gerd | کت دامن گرد |
| tuxedo | esmoking | اسموکینگ |

| uniform | oniform | اونیفورم |
| workwear | lebās-e kār | لباس کار |
| overalls | rupuš | روپوش |
| coat (e.g., doctor's smock) | rupuš | روپوش |

## 28. Clothing. Underwear

| underwear | lebās-e zir | لباس زیر |
| boxers, briefs | šort-e bākser | شورت باکسر |
| panties | šort-e zanāne | شورت زنانه |
| undershirt (A-shirt) | zir-e pirāhan-i | زیر پیراهنی |
| socks | jurāb | جوراب |

| nightgown | lebās-e xāb | لباس خواب |
| bra | sine-ye band | سینه بند |
| knee highs (knee-high socks) | sāq | ساق |
| pantyhose | jurāb-e šalvāri | جوراب شلواری |
| stockings (thigh highs) | jurāb-e sāqeboland | جوراب ساقه بلند |
| bathing suit | māyo | مایو |

## 29. Headwear

| hat | kolāh | کلاه |
| fedora | šāpo | شاپو |
| baseball cap | kolāh beysbāl | کلاه بیس بال |
| flatcap | kolāh-e taxt | کلاه تخت |

| beret | kolāh barre | کلاه بره |
| hood | kolāh-e bārāni | کلاه بارانی |
| panama hat | kolāh-e dowre-ye boland | کلاه دوره بلند |
| knit cap (knitted hat) | kolāh-e bāftani | کلاه بافتنی |

| headscarf | rusari | روسری |
| women's hat | kolāh-e zanāne | کلاه زنانه |
| hard hat | kolāh-e imeni | کلاه ایمنی |
| garrison cap | kolāh-e pādegān | کلاه پادگان |
| helmet | kolāh-e imeni | کلاه ایمنی |

| derby | kolāh-e namadi | کلاه نمدی |
| top hat | kolāh-e ostovānei | کلاه استوانه ای |

## 30. Footwear

| footwear | kafš | کفش |
| shoes (men's shoes) | putin | پوتین |

| shoes (women's shoes) | kafš | کفش |
| boots (e.g., cowboy ~) | čakme | چکمه |
| slippers | dampāyi | دمپایی |

| tennis shoes (e.g., Nike ~) | kafš katān-i | کفش کتانی |
| sneakers | kafš katān-i | کفش کتانی |
| (e.g., Converse ~) | | |
| sandals | sandal | صندل |

| cobbler (shoe repairer) | kaffāš | کفاش |
| heel | pāšne-ye kafš | پاشنهٔ کفش |
| pair (of shoes) | yek joft | یک جفت |

| shoestring | band-e kafš | بند کفش |
| to lace (vt) | band-e kafš bastan | بند کفش بستن |
| shoehorn | pāšne keš | پاشنه کش |
| shoe polish | vāks | واکس |

## 31. Personal accessories

| gloves | dastkeš | دستکش |
| mittens | dastkeš-e yek angošti | دستکش یک انگشتی |
| scarf (muffler) | šāl-e gardan | شال گردن |

| glasses (eyeglasses) | eynak | عینک |
| frame (eyeglass ~) | qāb | قاب |
| umbrella | čatr | چتر |
| walking stick | asā | عصا |

| hairbrush | bores-e mu | برس مو |
| fan | bādbezan | بادبزن |

| tie (necktie) | kerāvāt | کراوات |
| bow tie | pāpiyon | پاپیون |

| suspenders | band šalvār | بند شلوار |
| handkerchief | dastmāl | دستمال |

| comb | šāne | شانه |
| barrette | sanjāq-e mu | سنجاق مو |

| hairpin | sanjāq-e mu | سنجاق مو |
| buckle | sagak | سگک |

| belt | kamarband | کمربند |
| shoulder strap | tasme | تسمه |

| bag (handbag) | keyf | کیف |
| purse | keyf-e zanāne | کیف زنانه |
| backpack | kule pošti | کولهٔ پشتی |

## 32. Clothing. Miscellaneous

| | | |
|---|---|---|
| fashion | mod | مد |
| in vogue (adj) | mod | مد |
| fashion designer | tarrāh-e lebas | طراح لباس |
| | | |
| collar | yaqe | یقه |
| pocket | jib | جیب |
| pocket (as adj) | jibi | جیبی |
| sleeve | āstin | آستین |
| hanging loop | band-e āviz | بند آویز |
| fly (on trousers) | zip | زیپ |
| | | |
| zipper (fastener) | zip | زیپ |
| fastener | sagak | سگک |
| button | dokme | دکمه |
| buttonhole | surāx-e dokme | سوراخ دکمه |
| to come off (ab. button) | kande šodan | کنده شدن |
| | | |
| to sew (vi, vt) | duxtan | دوختن |
| to embroider (vi, vt) | golduzi kardan | گلدوزی کردن |
| embroidery | golduzi | گلدوزی |
| sewing needle | suzan | سوزن |
| thread | nax | نخ |
| seam | darz | درز |
| | | |
| to get dirty (vi) | kasif šodan | کثیف شدن |
| stain (mark, spot) | lakke | لکه |
| to crease, crumple (vi) | čoruk šodan | چروک شدن |
| to tear, to rip (vt) | pāre kardan | پاره کردن |
| clothes moth | šab parre | شب پره |

## 33. Personal care. Cosmetics

| | | |
|---|---|---|
| toothpaste | xamir-e dandān | خمیر دندان |
| toothbrush | mesvāk | مسواک |
| to brush one's teeth | mesvāk zadan | مسواک زدن |
| | | |
| razor | tiq | تیغ |
| shaving cream | kerem-e riš tarāši | کرم ریش تراشی |
| to shave (vi) | riš tarāšidan | ریش تراشیدن |
| | | |
| soap | sābun | صابون |
| shampoo | šāmpu | شامپو |
| | | |
| scissors | qeyči | قیچی |
| nail file | sohan-e nāxon | سوهان ناخن |
| nail clippers | nāxon gir | ناخن گیر |
| tweezers | mučin | موچین |

| cosmetics | lavāzem-e ārāyeši | لوازم آرایشی |
| face mask | māsk | ماسک |
| manicure | mānikur | مانیکور |
| to have a manicure | mānikur kardan | مانیکور کردن |
| pedicure | pedikur | پدیکور |

| make-up bag | kife lavāzem-e ārāyeši | کیف لوازم آرایشی |
| face powder | pudr | پودر |
| powder compact | ja'be-ye pudr | جعبهٔ پودر |
| blusher | sorxāb | سرخاب |

| perfume (bottled) | atr | عطر |
| toilet water (lotion) | atr | عطر |
| lotion | losiyon | لوسیون |
| cologne | odkolon | اودکلن |

| eyeshadow | sāye-ye češm | سایه چشم |
| eyeliner | medād čašm | مداد چشم |
| mascara | rimel | ریمل |

| lipstick | mātik | ماتیک |
| nail polish, enamel | lāk-e nāxon | لاک ناخن |
| hair spray | esperey-ye mu | اسپری مو |
| deodorant | deodyrant | دئودورانت |

| cream | kerem | کرم |
| face cream | kerem-e surat | کرم صورت |
| hand cream | kerem-e dast | کرم دست |
| anti-wrinkle cream | kerem-e zedd-e čoruk | کرم ضد چروک |
| day cream | kerem-e ruz | کرم روز |
| night cream | kerem-e šab | کرم شب |
| day (as adj) | ruzāne | روزانه |
| night (as adj) | šab | شب |

| tampon | tāmpon | تامپون |
| toilet paper (toilet roll) | kāqaz-e tuālet | کاغذ توالت |
| hair dryer | sešovār | سشوار |

## 34. Watches. Clocks

| watch (wristwatch) | sā'at-e moči | ساعت مچی |
| dial | safhe-ye sā'at | صفحهٔ ساعت |
| hand (of clock, watch) | aqrabe | عقربه |
| metal watch band | band-e sāat | بند ساعت |
| watch strap | band-e čarmi | بند چرمی |

| battery | bātri | باطری |
| to be dead (battery) | tamām šodan bātri | تمام شدن باتری |
| to change a battery | bātri avaz kardan | باطری عوض کردن |
| to run fast | jelo oftādan | جلو افتادن |

| to run slow | aqab māndan | عقب ماندن |
| wall clock | sā'at-e divāri | ساعت دیواری |
| hourglass | sā'at-e šeni | ساعت شنی |
| sundial | sā'at-e āftābi | ساعت آفتابی |
| alarm clock | sā'at-e zang dār | ساعت زنگ دار |
| watchmaker | sā'at sāz | ساعت ساز |
| to repair (vt) | ta'mir kardan | تعمیر کردن |

# Food. Nutricion

## 35. Food

| meat | gušt | گوشت |
|---|---|---|
| chicken | morq | مرغ |
| Rock Cornish hen (poussin) | juje | جوجه |
| duck | ordak | اردک |
| goose | qāz | غاز |
| game | gušt-e šekār | گوشت شکار |
| turkey | gušt-e buqalamun | گوشت بوقلمون |
| pork | gušt-e xuk | گوشت خوک |
| veal | gušt-e gusāle | گوشت گوساله |
| lamb | gušt-e gusfand | گوشت گوسفند |
| beef | gušt-e gāv | گوشت گاو |
| rabbit | xarguš | خرگوش |
| sausage (bologna, pepperoni, etc.) | kālbās | کالباس |
| vienna sausage (frankfurter) | sosis | سوسیس |
| bacon | beykon | بیکن |
| ham | žāmbon | ژامبون |
| gammon | rān xuk | ران خوک |
| pâté | pāte | پاته |
| liver | jegar | جگر |
| hamburger (ground beef) | hamberger | همبرگر |
| tongue | zabān | زبان |
| egg | toxm-e morq | تخم مرغ |
| eggs | toxm-e morq-ha | تخم مرغ ها |
| egg white | sefide-ye toxm-e morq | سفیده تخم مرغ |
| egg yolk | zarde-ye toxm-e morq | زرده تخم مرغ |
| fish | māhi | ماهی |
| seafood | qazā-ye daryāyi | غذای دریایی |
| crustaceans | saxtpustān | سختپوستان |
| caviar | xāviār | خاویار |
| crab | xarčang | خرچنگ |
| shrimp | meygu | میگو |
| oyster | sadaf-e xorāki | صدف خوراکی |
| spiny lobster | xarčang-e xārdār | خرچنگ خاردار |

| octopus | hašt pā | هشت پا |
| squid | māhi-ye morakkab | ماهی مرکب |

| sturgeon | māhi-ye xāviār | ماهی خاویار |
| salmon | māhi-ye salemon | ماهی سالمون |
| halibut | halibut | هالیبوت |

| cod | māhi-ye rowqan | ماهی روغن |
| mackerel | māhi-ye esqumeri | ماهی اسقومری |
| tuna | tan māhi | تن ماهی |
| eel | mārmāhi | مارماهی |

| trout | māhi-ye qezelālā | ماهی قزل آلا |
| sardine | sārdin | ساردین |
| pike | ordak māhi | اردک ماهی |
| herring | māhi-ye šur | ماهی شور |

| bread | nān | نان |
| cheese | panir | پنیر |
| sugar | qand | قند |
| salt | namak | نمک |

| rice | berenj | برنج |
| pasta (macaroni) | mākāroni | ماکارونی |
| noodles | rešte-ye farangi | رشته فرنگی |

| butter | kare | کره |
| vegetable oil | rowqan-e nabāti | روغن نباتی |
| sunflower oil | rowqan āftābgardān | روغن آفتاب گردان |
| margarine | mārgārin | مارگارین |

| olives | zeytun | زیتون |
| olive oil | rowqan-e zeytun | روغن زیتون |

| milk | šir | شیر |
| condensed milk | šir-e čegāl | شیر چگال |
| yogurt | mās-at | ماست |

| sour cream | xāme-ye torš | خامۀ ترش |
| cream (of milk) | saršir | سرشیر |

| mayonnaise | māyonez | مایونز |
| buttercream | xāme | خامه |

| cereal grains (wheat, etc.) | hobubāt | حبوبات |
| flour | ārd | آرد |
| canned food | konserv-hā | کنسرو ها |

| cornflakes | bereštuk | برشتوک |
| honey | asal | عسل |
| jam | morabbā | مربا |
| chewing gum | ādāms | آدامس |

## 36. Drinks

| water | āb | آب |
| drinking water | āb-e āšāmidani | آب آشامیدنی |
| mineral water | āb-e ma'dani | آب معدنی |

| still (adj) | bedun-e gāz | بدون گاز |
| carbonated (adj) | gāzdār | گازدار |
| sparkling (adj) | gāzdār | گازدار |
| ice | yax | یخ |
| with ice | yax dār | یخ دار |

| non-alcoholic (adj) | bi alkol | بی الکل |
| soft drink | nušābe-ye bi alkol | نوشابۀ بی الکل |
| refreshing drink | nušābe-ye xonak | نوشابۀ خنک |
| lemonade | limunād | لیموناد |

| liquors | mašrubāt-e alkoli | مشروبات الکلی |
| wine | šarāb | شراب |
| white wine | šarāb-e sefid | شراب سفید |
| red wine | šarāb-e sorx | شراب سرخ |

| liqueur | likor | لیکور |
| champagne | šāmpāyn | شامپاین |
| vermouth | vermut | ورموت |

| whiskey | viski | ویسکی |
| vodka | vodkā | ودکا |
| gin | jin | جین |
| cognac | konyāk | کنیاک |
| rum | araq-e neyšekar | عرق نیشکر |

| coffee | qahve | قهوه |
| black coffee | qahve-ye talx | قهوۀ تلخ |
| coffee with milk | šir-qahve | شیرقهوه |
| cappuccino | kāpočino | کاپوچینو |
| instant coffee | qahve-ye fowri | قهوه فوری |

| milk | šir | شیر |
| cocktail | kuktel | کوکتل |
| milkshake | kuktele šir | کوکتل شیر |

| juice | āb-e mive | آب میوه |
| tomato juice | āb-e gowjefarangi | آب گوجه فرنگی |
| orange juice | āb-e porteqāl | آب پرتقال |
| freshly squeezed juice | āb-e mive-ye taze | آب میوۀ تازه |

| beer | ābejow | آبجو |
| light beer | ābejow-ye sabok | آبجوی سبک |
| dark beer | ābejow-ye tire | آبجوی تیره |
| tea | čāy | چای |

| black tea | čāy-e siyāh | چای سیاه |
| green tea | čāy-e sabz | چای سبز |

## 37. Vegetables

| vegetables | sabzijāt | سبزیجات |
| greens | sabzi | سبزی |

| tomato | gowje farangi | گوجه فرنگی |
| cucumber | xiyār | خیار |
| carrot | havij | هویج |
| potato | sib zamini | سیب زمینی |
| onion | piyāz | پیاز |
| garlic | sir | سیر |

| cabbage | kalam | کلم |
| cauliflower | gol kalam | گل کلم |
| Brussels sprouts | koll-am boruksel | کلم بروکسل |
| broccoli | kalam borokli | کلم بروکلی |

| beetroot | čoqondar | چغندر |
| eggplant | bādenjān | بادنجان |
| zucchini | kadu sabz | کدو سبز |
| pumpkin | kadu tanbal | کدو تنبل |
| turnip | šalqam | شلغم |

| parsley | ja'fari | جعفری |
| dill | šavid | شوید |
| lettuce | kāhu | کاهو |
| celery | karafs | کرفس |
| asparagus | mārčube | مارچوبه |
| spinach | esfenāj | اسفناج |

| pea | noxod | نخود |
| beans | lubiyā | لوبیا |
| corn (maize) | zorrat | ذرت |
| kidney bean | lubiyā qermez | لوبیا قرمز |

| bell pepper | felfel | فلفل |
| radish | torobče | تربچه |
| artichoke | kangar farangi | کنگرفرنگی |

## 38. Fruits. Nuts

| fruit | mive | میوه |
| apple | sib | سیب |
| pear | golābi | گلابی |
| lemon | limu | لیمو |

| orange | porteqāl | پرتقال |
| strawberry (garden ~) | tut-e farangi | توت فرنگی |

| mandarin | nārengi | نارنگی |
| plum | ālu | آلو |
| peach | holu | هلو |
| apricot | zardālu | زردآلو |
| raspberry | tamešk | تمشک |
| pineapple | ānānās | آناناس |

| banana | mowz | موز |
| watermelon | hendevāne | هندوانه |
| grape | angur | انگور |
| sour cherry | ālbālu | آلبالو |
| sweet cherry | gilās | گیلاس |
| melon | xarboze | خربزه |

| grapefruit | gerip forut | گریپ فوروت |
| avocado | āvokādo | اووکادو |
| papaya | pāpāyā | پاپایا |
| mango | anbe | انبه |
| pomegranate | anār | انار |

| redcurrant | angur-e farangi-ye sorx | انگور فرنگی سرخ |
| blackcurrant | angur-e farangi-ye siyāh | انگور فرنگی سیاه |
| gooseberry | angur-e farangi | انگور فرنگی |
| bilberry | zoqāl axte | زغال اخته |
| blackberry | šāh tut | شاه توت |

| raisin | kešmeš | کشمش |
| fig | anjir | انجیر |
| date | xormā | خرما |

| peanut | bādām zamin-i | بادام زمینی |
| almond | bādām | بادام |
| walnut | gerdu | گردو |
| hazelnut | fandoq | فندق |
| coconut | nārgil | نارگیل |
| pistachios | peste | پسته |

## 39. Bread. Candy

| bakers' confectionery (pastry) | širini jāt | شیرینی جات |
| bread | nān | نان |
| cookies | biskuit | بیسکوییت |

| chocolate (n) | šokolāt | شکلات |
| chocolate (as adj) | šokolāti | شکلاتی |
| candy (wrapped) | āb nabāt | آب نبات |

| cake (e.g., cupcake) | nān-e širini | نان شیرینی |
| cake (e.g., birthday ~) | širini | شیرینی |
| | | |
| pie (e.g., apple ~) | keyk | کیک |
| filling (for cake, pie) | čāšni | چاشنی |
| | | |
| jam (whole fruit jam) | morabbā | مربا |
| marmalade | mārmālād | مارمالاد |
| waffles | vāfel | وافل |
| ice-cream | bastani | بستنی |
| pudding | puding | پودینگ |

## 40. Cooked dishes

| course, dish | qazā | غذا |
| cuisine | qazā | غذا |
| recipe | dastur-e poxt | دستور پخت |
| portion | pors | پرس |
| | | |
| salad | sālād | سالاد |
| soup | sup | سوپ |
| | | |
| clear soup (broth) | pāye-ye sup | پایه سوپ |
| sandwich (bread) | sāndevič | ساندویچ |
| fried eggs | nimru | نیمرو |
| | | |
| hamburger (beefburger) | hamberger | همبرگر |
| beefsteak | esteyk | استیک |
| | | |
| side dish | moxallafāt | مخلفات |
| spaghetti | espāgeti | اسپاگتی |
| mashed potatoes | pure-ye sibi zamini | پورۀ سیب زمینی |
| pizza | pitzā | پیتزا |
| porridge (oatmeal, etc.) | šurbā | شوربا |
| omelet | ommol-at | املت |
| | | |
| boiled (e.g., ~ beef) | āb paz | آب پز |
| smoked (adj) | dudi | دودی |
| fried (adj) | sorx šode | سرخ شده |
| dried (adj) | xošk | خشک |
| frozen (adj) | yax zade | یخ زده |
| pickled (adj) | torši | ترشی |
| | | |
| sweet (sugary) | širin | شیرین |
| salty (adj) | šur | شور |
| cold (adj) | sard | سرد |
| hot (adj) | dāq | داغ |
| bitter (adj) | talx | تلخ |
| tasty (adj) | xoš mazze | خوش مزه |
| to cook in boiling water | poxtan | پختن |

| to cook (dinner) | poxtan | پختن |
| to fry (vt) | sorx kardan | سرخ کردن |
| to heat up (food) | garm kardan | گرم کردن |

| to salt (vt) | namak zadan | نمک زدن |
| to pepper (vt) | felfel pāšidan | فلفل پاشیدن |
| to grate (vt) | rande kardan | رنده کردن |
| peel (n) | pust | پوست |
| to peel (vt) | pust kandan | پوست کندن |

## 41. Spices

| salt | namak | نمک |
| salty (adj) | šur | شور |
| to salt (vt) | namak zadan | نمک زدن |

| black pepper | felfel-e siyāh | فلفل سیاه |
| red pepper (milled ~) | felfel-e sorx | فلفل سرخ |
| mustard | xardal | خردل |
| horseradish | torob-e kuhi | ترب کوهی |

| condiment | adviye | ادویه |
| spice | adviye | ادویه |
| sauce | ses | سس |
| vinegar | serke | سرکه |

| anise | rāziyāne | رازیانه |
| basil | reyhān | ریحان |
| cloves | mixak | میخک |
| ginger | zanjefil | زنجفیل |
| coriander | gešniz | گشنیز |
| cinnamon | dārčin | دارچین |

| sesame | konjed | کنجد |
| bay leaf | barg-e bu | برگ بو |
| paprika | paprika | پاپریکا |
| caraway | zire | زیره |
| saffron | za'ferān | زعفران |

## 42. Meals

| food | qazā | غذا |
| to eat (vi, vt) | xordan | خوردن |

| breakfast | sobhāne | صبحانه |
| to have breakfast | sobhāne xordan | صبحانه خوردن |
| lunch | nāhār | ناهار |
| to have lunch | nāhār xordan | ناهار خوردن |

| dinner | šām | شام |
| to have dinner | šām xordan | شام خوردن |

| appetite | eštehā | اشتها |
| Enjoy your meal! | nuš-e jān | نوش جان |

| to open (~ a bottle) | bāz kardan | باز کردن |
| to spill (liquid) | rixtan | ریختن |
| to spill out (vi) | rixtan | ریختن |

| to boil (vi) | jušidan | جوشیدن |
| to boil (vt) | jušāndan | جوشاندن |
| boiled (~ water) | jušide | جوشیده |

| to chill, cool down (vt) | sard kardan | سرد کردن |
| to chill (vi) | sard šodan | سرد شدن |

| taste, flavor | maze | مزه |
| aftertaste | maze | مزه |

| to slim down (lose weight) | lāqar kardan | لاغر کردن |
| diet | režim | رژیم |

| vitamin | vitāmin | ویتامین |
| calorie | kālori | کالری |

| vegetarian (n) | giyāh xār | گیاه خوار |
| vegetarian (adj) | giyāh xāri | گیاه خواری |

| fats (nutrient) | čarbi-hā | چربی ها |
| proteins | porotein | پروتئین |
| carbohydrates | karbohidrāt-hā | کربو هیدرات ها |

| slice (of lemon, ham) | qet'e | قطعه |
| piece (of cake, pie) | tekke | تکه |
| crumb | zarre | ذره |
| (of bread, cake, etc.) | | |

## 43. Table setting

| spoon | qāšoq | قاشق |
| knife | kārd | کارد |
| fork | čangāl | چنگال |

| cup (e.g., coffee ~) | fenjān | فنجان |
| plate (dinner ~) | bošqāb | بشقاب |

| saucer | na'lbeki | نعلبکی |
| napkin (on table) | dastmāl | دستمال |
| toothpick | xelāl-e dandān | خلال دندان |

## 44. Restaurant

| | | |
|---|---|---|
| restaurant | resturān | رستوران |
| coffee house | kāfe | کافه |
| pub, bar | bār | بار |
| tearoom | qahve xāne | قهوه خانه |
| | | |
| waiter | pišxedmat | پیشخدمت |
| waitress | pišxedmat | پیشخدمت |
| bartender | motesaddi-ye bār | متصدی بار |
| | | |
| menu | meno | منو |
| wine list | kārt-e šarāb | کارت شراب |
| to book a table | miz rezerv kardan | میز رزرو کردن |
| | | |
| course, dish | qazā | غذا |
| to order (meal) | sefāreš dādan | سفارش دادن |
| to make an order | sefāreš dādan | سفارش دادن |
| | | |
| aperitif | mašrub-e piš qazā | مشروب پیش غذا |
| appetizer | piš qazā | پیش غذا |
| dessert | deser | دسر |
| | | |
| check | surat hesāb | صورت حساب |
| to pay the check | surat-e hesāb rā pardāxtan | صورت حساب را پرداختن |
| | | |
| to give change | baqiye rā dādan | بقیه را دادن |
| tip | an'ām | انعام |

# Family, relatives and friends

## 45. Personal information. Forms

| | | |
|---|---|---|
| name (first name) | esm | اسم |
| surname (last name) | nām-e xānevādegi | نام خانوادگی |
| date of birth | tārix-e tavallod | تاریخ تولد |
| place of birth | mahall-e tavallod | محل تولد |
| | | |
| nationality | melliyat | ملیت |
| place of residence | mahall-e sokunat | محل سکونت |
| country | kešvar | کشور |
| profession (occupation) | šoql | شغل |
| | | |
| gender, sex | jens | جنس |
| height | qad | قد |
| weight | vazn | وزن |

## 46. Family members. Relatives

| | | |
|---|---|---|
| mother | mādar | مادر |
| father | pedar | پدر |
| son | pesar | پسر |
| daughter | doxtar | دختر |
| | | |
| younger daughter | doxtar-e kučak | دختر کوچک |
| younger son | pesar-e kučak | پسر کوچک |
| eldest daughter | doxtar-e bozorg | دختر بزرگ |
| eldest son | pesar-e bozorg | پسر بزرگ |
| | | |
| brother | barādar | برادر |
| elder brother | barādar-e bozorg | برادر بزرگ |
| younger brother | barādar-e kučak | برادر کوچک |
| sister | xāhar | خواهر |
| elder sister | xāhar-e bozorg | خواهر بزرگ |
| younger sister | xāhar-e kučak | خواهر کوچک |
| | | |
| cousin (masc.) | pesar 'amu | پسر عمو |
| cousin (fem.) | doxtar amu | دختر عمو |
| | | |
| mom, mommy | māmān | مامان |
| dad, daddy | bābā | بابا |
| parents | vāledeyn | والدین |
| child | kudak | کودک |

53

| children | bače-hā | بچه ها |
| grandmother | mādarbozorg | مادربزرگ |
| grandfather | pedar-bozorg | پدربزرگ |
| grandson | nave | نوه |
| granddaughter | nave | نوه |
| grandchildren | nave-hā | نوه ها |

| uncle | amu | عمو |
| aunt | xāle yā amme | خاله یا عمه |
| nephew | barādar-zāde | برادرزاده |
| niece | xāhar-zāde | خواهرزاده |

| mother-in-law (wife's mother) | mādarzan | مادرزن |
| father-in-law (husband's father) | pedar-šowhar | پدرشوهر |
| son-in-law (daughter's husband) | dāmād | داماد |
| stepmother | nāmādari | نامادری |
| stepfather | nāpedari | ناپدری |

| infant | nowzād | نوزاد |
| baby (infant) | širxār | شیرخوار |
| little boy, kid | pesar-e kučulu | پسر کوچولو |

| wife | zan | زن |
| husband | šowhar | شوهر |
| spouse (husband) | hamsar | همسر |
| spouse (wife) | hamsar | همسر |

| married (masc.) | mote'ahhel | متاهل |
| married (fem.) | mote'ahhel | متاهل |
| single (unmarried) | mojarrad | مجرد |
| bachelor | mojarrad | مجرد |
| divorced (masc.) | talāq gerefte | طلاق گرفته |
| widow | bive zan | بیوه زن |
| widower | bive | بیوه |

| relative | xišāvand | خویشاوند |
| close relative | aqvām-e nazdik | اقوام نزدیک |
| distant relative | aqvām-e dur | اقوام دور |
| relatives | aqvām | اقوام |

| orphan (boy or girl) | yatim | یتیم |
| guardian (of a minor) | qayyem | قیم |
| to adopt (a boy) | be pesari gereftan | به پسری گرفتن |
| to adopt (a girl) | be doxtari gereftan | به دختری گرفتن |

# Medicine

## 47. Diseases

| | | |
|---|---|---|
| sickness | bimāri | بیماری |
| to be sick | bimār budan | بیمار بودن |
| health | salāmati | سلامتی |
| | | |
| runny nose (coryza) | āb-e rizeš-e bini | آب ریزش بینی |
| tonsillitis | varam-e lowze | ورم لوزه |
| cold (illness) | sarmā xordegi | سرما خوردگی |
| to catch a cold | sarmā xordan | سرما خوردن |
| | | |
| bronchitis | boronšit | برنشیت |
| pneumonia | zātorrie | ذات الریه |
| flu, influenza | ānfolānzā | آنفولانزا |
| | | |
| nearsighted (adj) | nazdik bin | نزدیک بین |
| farsighted (adj) | durbin | دوربین |
| strabismus (crossed eyes) | enherāf-e čašm | انحراف چشم |
| cross-eyed (adj) | luč | لوچ |
| cataract | āb morvārid | آب مروارید |
| glaucoma | ab-e siyāh | آب سیاه |
| | | |
| stroke | sekte-ye maqzi | سکته مغزی |
| heart attack | sekte-ye qalbi | سکته قلبی |
| myocardial infarction | ānfārktus | آنفارکتوس |
| paralysis | falaji | فلجی |
| to paralyze (vt) | falj kardan | فلج کردن |
| | | |
| allergy | ālerži | آلرژی |
| asthma | āsm | آسم |
| diabetes | diyābet | دیابت |
| | | |
| toothache | dandān-e dard | دندان درد |
| caries | pusidegi | پوسیدگی |
| | | |
| diarrhea | eshāl | اسهال |
| constipation | yobusat | یبوست |
| stomach upset | nārāhati-ye me'de | ناراحتی معده |
| food poisoning | masmumiyat | مسمومیت |
| to get food poisoning | masmum šodan | مسموم شدن |
| | | |
| arthritis | varam-e mafāsel | ورم مفاصل |
| rickets | rāšitism | راشیتیسم |
| rheumatism | romātism | روماتیسم |

| atherosclerosis | tasallob-e šarāin | تصلب شرائین |
| gastritis | varam-e me'de | ورم معده |
| appendicitis | āpāndisit | آپاندیسیت |
| cholecystitis | eltehāb-e kise-ye safrā | التهاب کیسه صفرا |
| ulcer | zaxm | زخم |

| measles | sorxak | سرخک |
| rubella (German measles) | sorxje | سرخجه |
| jaundice | yaraqān | یرقان |
| hepatitis | hepātit | هپاتیت |

| schizophrenia | šizoferni | شیزوفرنی |
| rabies (hydrophobia) | hāri | هاری |
| neurosis | extelāl-e a'sāb | اختلال اعصاب |
| concussion | zarbe-ye maqzi | ضربه مغزی |

| cancer | saratān | سرطان |
| sclerosis | eskeleroz | اسکلروز |
| multiple sclerosis | eskeleroz čandgāne | اسکلروز چندگانه |

| alcoholism | alkolism | الکلیسم |
| alcoholic (n) | alkoli | الکلی |
| syphilis | siflis | سیفلیس |
| AIDS | eydz | ایدز |

| tumor | tumor | تومور |
| malignant (adj) | bad xim | بد خیم |
| benign (adj) | xoš xim | خوش خیم |

| fever | tab | تب |
| malaria | mālāriyā | مالاریا |
| gangrene | qānqāriyā | قانقاریا |
| seasickness | daryā-zadegi | دریازدگی |
| epilepsy | sar' | صرع |

| epidemic | epidemi | اپیدمی |
| typhus | hasbe | حصبه |
| tuberculosis | sel | سل |
| cholera | vabā | وبا |
| plague (bubonic ~) | tā'un | طاعون |

## 48. Symptoms. Treatments. Part 1

| symptom | alāem-e bimāri | علائم بیماری |
| temperature | damā | دما |
| high temperature (fever) | tab | تب |
| pulse | nabz | نبض |

| dizziness (vertigo) | sargije | سرگیجه |
| hot (adj) | dāq | داغ |

| | | |
|---|---|---|
| shivering | ra'še | رعشه |
| pale (e.g., ~ face) | rang paride | رنگ پریده |
| | | |
| cough | sorfe | سرفه |
| to cough (vi) | sorfe kardan | سرفه کردن |
| to sneeze (vi) | atse kardan | عطسه کردن |
| faint | qaš | غش |
| to faint (vi) | qaš kardan | غش کردن |
| | | |
| bruise (hématome) | kabudi | کبودی |
| bump (lump) | barāmadegi | برآمدگی |
| to bang (bump) | barxord kardan | برخورد کردن |
| contusion (bruise) | kuftegi | کوفتگی |
| to get a bruise | zarb didan | ضرب دیدن |
| | | |
| to limp (vi) | langidan | لنگیدن |
| dislocation | dar raftegi | دررفتگی |
| to dislocate (vt) | dar raftan | دررفتن |
| fracture | šekastegi | شکستگی |
| to have a fracture | dočār-e šekastegi šodan | دچار شکستگی شدن |
| | | |
| cut (e.g., paper ~) | boridegi | بریدگی |
| to cut oneself | boridan | بریدن |
| bleeding | xunrizi | خونریزی |
| | | |
| burn (injury) | suxtegi | سوختگی |
| to get burned | dočār-e suxtegi šodan | دچار سوختگی شدن |
| | | |
| to prick (vt) | surāx kardan | سوراخ کردن |
| to prick oneself | surāx kardan | سوراخ کردن |
| to injure (vt) | āsib resāndan | آسیب رساندن |
| injury | zaxm | زخم |
| wound | zaxm | زخم |
| trauma | zarbe | ضربه |
| | | |
| to be delirious | hazyān goftan | هذیان گفتن |
| to stutter (vi) | loknat dāštan | لکنت داشتن |
| sunstroke | āftāb-zadegi | آفتابزدگی |

## 49. Symptoms. Treatments. Part 2

| | | |
|---|---|---|
| pain, ache | dard | درد |
| splinter (in foot, etc.) | xār | خار |
| | | |
| sweat (perspiration) | araq | عرق |
| to sweat (perspire) | araq kardan | عرق کردن |
| vomiting | estefrāq | استفراغ |
| convulsions | tašannoj | تشنج |
| pregnant (adj) | bārdār | باردار |
| to be born | motevalled šodan | متولد شدن |

| delivery, labor | vaz'-e haml | وضع حمل |
| to deliver (~ a baby) | be donyā āvardan | به دنیا آوردن |
| abortion | seqt-e janin | سقط جنین |

| breathing, respiration | tanaffos | تنفس |
| in-breath (inhalation) | estenšāq | استنشاق |
| out-breath (exhalation) | bāzdam | بازدم |
| to exhale (breathe out) | bāzdamidan | بازدمیدن |
| to inhale (vi) | nafas kešidan | نفس کشیدن |

| disabled person | ma'lul | معلول |
| cripple | falaj | فلج |
| drug addict | mo'tād | معتاد |

| deaf (adj) | kar | کر |
| mute (adj) | lāl | لال |
| deaf mute (adj) | kar-o lāl | کر و لال |

| mad, insane (adj) | divāne | دیوانه |
| madman (demented person) | divāne | دیوانه |
| madwoman | divāne | دیوانه |
| to go insane | divāne šodan | دیوانه شدن |

| gene | žen | ژن |
| immunity | masuniyat | مصونیت |
| hereditary (adj) | mowrusi | موروثی |
| congenital (adj) | mādarzād | مادرزاد |

| virus | virus | ویروس |
| microbe | mikrob | میکروب |
| bacterium | bākteri | باکتری |
| infection | ofunat | عفونت |

## 50. Symptoms. Treatments. Part 3

| hospital | bimārestān | بیمارستان |
| patient | bimār | بیمار |

| diagnosis | tašxis | تشخیص |
| cure | mo'āleje | معالجه |
| medical treatment | darmān | درمان |
| to get treatment | darmān šodan | درمان شدن |
| to treat (~ a patient) | mo'āleje kardan | معالجه کردن |
| to nurse (look after) | parastāri kardan | پرستاری کردن |
| care (nursing ~) | parastāri | پرستاری |

| operation, surgery | amal-e jarrāhi | عمل جراحی |
| to bandage (head, limb) | pānsemān kardan | پانسمان کردن |
| bandaging | pānsemān | پانسمان |

| | | |
|---|---|---|
| vaccination | vāksināsyon | واکسیناسیون |
| to vaccinate (vt) | vāksine kardan | واکسینه کردن |
| injection, shot | tazriq | تزریق |
| to give an injection | tazriq kardan | تزریق کردن |

| | | |
|---|---|---|
| attack | hamle | حمله |
| amputation | qat'-e ozv | قطع عضو |
| to amputate (vt) | qat' kardan | قطع کردن |
| coma | komā | کما |
| to be in a coma | dar komā budan | در کما بودن |
| intensive care | morāqebat-e viže | مراقبت ویژه |

| | | |
|---|---|---|
| to recover (~ from flu) | behbud yāftan | بهبود یافتن |
| condition (patient's ~) | hālat | حالت |
| consciousness | huš | هوش |
| memory (faculty) | hāfeze | حافظه |

| | | |
|---|---|---|
| to pull out (tooth) | dandān kešidan | دندان کشیدن |
| filling | por kardan | پر کردن |
| to fill (a tooth) | por kardan | پر کردن |

| | | |
|---|---|---|
| hypnosis | hipnotizm | هیپنوتیزم |
| to hypnotize (vt) | hipnotizm kardan | هیپنوتیزم کردن |

## 51. Doctors

| | | |
|---|---|---|
| doctor | pezešk | پزشک |
| nurse | parastār | پرستار |
| personal doctor | pezešk-e šaxsi | پزشک شخصی |

| | | |
|---|---|---|
| dentist | dandān pezešk | دندان پزشک |
| eye doctor | češm-pezešk | چشم پزشک |
| internist | pezešk omumi | پزشک عمومی |
| surgeon | jarrāh | جراح |

| | | |
|---|---|---|
| psychiatrist | ravānpezešk | روانپزشک |
| pediatrician | pezešk-e kudakān | پزشک کودکان |
| psychologist | ravānšenās | روانشناس |
| gynecologist | motexasses-e zanān | متخصص زنان |
| cardiologist | motexasses-e qalb | متخصص قلب |

## 52. Medicine. Drugs. Accessories

| | | |
|---|---|---|
| medicine, drug | dāru | دارو |
| remedy | darmān | درمان |
| to prescribe (vt) | tajviz kardan | تجویز کردن |
| prescription | nosxe | نسخه |
| tablet, pill | qors | قرص |

| ointment | pomād | پماد |
| ampule | āmpul | آمپول |
| mixture | šarbat | شربت |
| syrup | šarbat | شربت |
| pill | kapsul | کپسول |
| powder | pudr | پودر |

| gauze bandage | bānd | باند |
| cotton wool | panbe | پنبه |
| iodine | yod | ید |

| Band-Aid | časb-e zaxm | چسب زخم |
| eyedropper | qatre čekān | قطره چکان |
| thermometer | damāsanj | دماسنج |
| syringe | sorang | سرنگ |

| wheelchair | vilčer | ویلچر |
| crutches | čub zir baqal | چوب زیر بغل |

| painkiller | mosaken | مسکن |
| laxative | moshel | مسهل |
| spirits (ethanol) | alkol | الکل |
| medicinal herbs | giyāhān-e dāruyi | گیاهان دارویی |
| herbal (~ tea) | giyāhi | گیاهی |

# HUMAN HABITAT

## City

### 53. City. Life in the city

| city, town | šahr | شهر |
| capital city | pāytaxt | پایتخت |
| village | rustā | روستا |

| city map | naqše-ye šahr | نقشهٔ شهر |
| downtown | markaz-e šahr | مرکز شهر |
| suburb | hume-ye šahr | حومهٔ شهر |
| suburban (adj) | hume-ye šahr | حومهٔ شهر |

| outskirts | hume | حومه |
| environs (suburbs) | hume | حومه |
| city block | mahalle | محله |
| residential block (area) | mahalle-ye maskuni | محلهٔ مسکونی |

| traffic | obur-o morur | عبور و مرور |
| traffic lights | čerāq-e rāhnamā | چراغ راهنما |
| public transportation | haml-o naql-e šahri | حمل و نقل شهری |
| intersection | čahārrāh | چهارراه |

| crosswalk | xatt-e āber-e piyāde | خط عابرپیاده |
| pedestrian underpass | zir-e gozar | زیر گذر |
| to cross (~ the street) | obur kardan | عبور کردن |
| pedestrian | piyāde | پیاده |
| sidewalk | piyāde row | پیاده رو |

| bridge | pol | پل |
| embankment (river walk) | xiyābān-e sāheli | خیابان ساحلی |
| fountain | češme | چشمه |

| allée (garden walkway) | bāq rāh | باغ راه |
| park | pārk | پارک |
| boulevard | bolvār | بولوار |
| square | meydān | میدان |
| avenue (wide street) | xiyābān | خیابان |
| street | xiyābān | خیابان |
| side street | kuče | کوچه |
| dead end | bon bast | بن بست |
| house | xāne | خانه |
| building | sāxtemān | ساختمان |

| skyscraper | āsemānxarāš | آسمانخراش |
| facade | namā | نما |
| roof | bām | بام |
| window | panjere | پنجره |
| arch | tāq-e qowsi | طاق قوسی |
| column | sotun | ستون |
| corner | nabš | نبش |

| store window | vitrin | ویترین |
| signboard (store sign, etc.) | tāblo | تابلو |
| poster | poster | پوستر |
| advertising poster | poster-e tabliqāti | پوستر تبلیغاتی |
| billboard | bilbord | بیلبورد |

| garbage, trash | āšqāl | آشغال |
| trashcan (public ~) | satl-e āšqāl | سطل آشغال |
| to litter (vi) | kasif kardan | کثیف کردن |
| garbage dump | jā-ye dafn-e āšqāl | جای دفن آشغال |

| phone booth | kābin-e telefon | کابین تلفن |
| lamppost | tir-e barq | تیر برق |
| bench (park ~) | nimkat | نیمکت |

| police officer | polis | پلیس |
| police | polis | پلیس |
| beggar | gedā | گدا |
| homeless (n) | bi xānomān | بی خانمان |

## 54. Urban institutions

| store | maqāze | مغازه |
| drugstore, pharmacy | dāruxāne | داروخانه |
| eyeglass store | eynak foruši | عینک فروشی |
| shopping mall | markaz-e tejāri | مرکز تجاری |
| supermarket | supermārket | سوپرمارکت |

| bakery | nānvāyi | نانوایی |
| baker | nānvā | نانوا |
| pastry shop | qannādi | قنادی |
| grocery store | baqqāli | بقالی |
| butcher shop | gušt foruši | گوشت فروشی |

| produce store | sabzi foruši | سبزی فروشی |
| market | bāzār | بازار |

| coffee house | kāfe | کافه |
| restaurant | resturān | رستوران |
| pub, bar | bār | بار |
| pizzeria | pitzā-foruši | پیتزا فروشی |
| hair salon | ārāyešgāh | آرایشگاه |

| | | |
|---|---|---|
| post office | post | پست |
| dry cleaners | xošk-šuyi | خشک‌شویی |
| photo studio | ātolye-ye akkāsi | آتلیهٔ عکاسی |
| | | |
| shoe store | kafš foruši | کفش فروشی |
| bookstore | ketāb-foruši | کتاب فروشی |
| sporting goods store | maqāze-ye varzeši | مغازهٔ ورزشی |
| | | |
| clothes repair shop | ta'mir-e lebās | تعمیر لباس |
| formal wear rental | kerāye-ye lebās | کرایهٔ لباس |
| video rental store | kerāye-ye film | کرایهٔ فیلم |
| | | |
| circus | sirak | سیرک |
| zoo | bāq-e vahš | باغ وحش |
| movie theater | sinamā | سینما |
| museum | muze | موزه |
| library | ketābxāne | کتابخانه |
| | | |
| theater | teātr | تئاتر |
| opera (opera house) | operā | اپرا |
| | | |
| nightclub | kābāre | کاباره |
| casino | kāzino | کازینو |
| | | |
| mosque | masjed | مسجد |
| synagogue | kenešt | کنشت |
| cathedral | kelisā-ye jāme' | کلیسای جامع |
| | | |
| temple | ma'bad | معبد |
| church | kelisā | کلیسا |
| | | |
| college | anistito | انستیتو |
| university | dānešgāh | دانشگاه |
| school | madrese | مدرسه |
| | | |
| prefecture | ostāndāri | استانداری |
| city hall | šahrdāri | شهرداری |
| | | |
| hotel | hotel | هتل |
| bank | bānk | بانک |
| | | |
| embassy | sefārat | سفارت |
| travel agency | āžāns-e jahāngardi | آژانس جهانگردی |
| | | |
| information office | daftar-e ettelāāt | دفتر اطلاعات |
| currency exchange | sarrāfi | صرافی |
| | | |
| subway | metro | مترو |
| hospital | bimārestān | بیمارستان |
| | | |
| gas station | pomp-e benzin | پمپ بنزین |
| parking lot | pārking | پارکینگ |

## 55. Signs

| | | |
|---|---|---|
| signboard (store sign, etc.) | tāblo | تابلو |
| notice (door sign, etc.) | nevešte | نوشته |
| poster | poster | پوستر |
| direction sign | rāhnamā | راهنما |
| arrow (sign) | alāmat | علامت |
| | | |
| caution | ehtiyāt | احتیاط |
| warning sign | alāmat-e hošdār | علامت هشدار |
| to warn (vt) | hošdār dādan | هشدار دادن |
| | | |
| rest day (weekly ~) | ruz-e ta'til | روز تعطیل |
| timetable (schedule) | jadval | جدول |
| opening hours | sā'athā-ye kāri | ساعت های کاری |
| | | |
| WELCOME! | xoš āmadid | خوش آمدید |
| ENTRANCE | vorud | ورود |
| EXIT | xoruj | خروج |
| | | |
| PUSH | hel dādan | هل دادن |
| PULL | bekešid | بکشید |
| OPEN | bāz | باز |
| CLOSED | baste | بسته |
| | | |
| WOMEN | zanāne | زنانه |
| MEN | mardāne | مردانه |
| | | |
| DISCOUNTS | taxfif | تخفیف |
| SALE | harāj | حراج |
| NEW! | jadid | جدید |
| FREE | majjāni | مجانی |
| | | |
| ATTENTION! | tavajjoh | توجه |
| NO VACANCIES | otāq-e xāli nadārim | اتاق خالی نداریم |
| RESERVED | rezerv šode | رزرو شده |
| | | |
| ADMINISTRATION | edāre | اداره |
| STAFF ONLY | xāse personel | خاص پرسنل |
| | | |
| BEWARE OF THE DOG! | movāzeb-e sag bāšid | مواظب سگ باشید |
| NO SMOKING | sigār kešidan mamnu' | سیگار کشیدن ممنوع |
| DO NOT TOUCH! | dast nazanid | دست نزنید |
| | | |
| DANGEROUS | xatarnāk | خطرناک |
| DANGER | xatar | خطر |
| HIGH VOLTAGE | voltāj bālā | ولتاژ بالا |
| NO SWIMMING! | šenā mamnu' | شنا ممنوع |
| OUT OF ORDER | xārāb | خراب |
| FLAMMABLE | qābel-e ehterāq | قابل احتراق |
| FORBIDDEN | mamnu' | ممنوع |

| NO TRESPASSING! | obur mamnu' | عبور ممنوع |
| WET PAINT | rang-e xis | رنگ خیس |

## 56. Urban transportation

| bus | otobus | اتوبوس |
| streetcar | terāmvā | تراموا |
| trolley bus | otobus-e barqi | اتوبوس برقی |
| route (of bus, etc.) | xat | خط |
| number (e.g., bus ~) | šomāre | شماره |

| to go by ... | raftan bā | رفتن با |
| to get on (~ the bus) | savār šodan | سوار شدن |
| to get off ... | piyāde šodan | پیاده شدن |

| stop (e.g., bus ~) | istgāh-e otobus | ایستگاه اتوبوس |
| next stop | istgāh-e ba'di | ایستگاه بعدی |
| terminus | istgāh-e āxar | ایستگاه آخر |
| schedule | barnāme | برنامه |
| to wait (vt) | montazer budan | منتظر بودن |

| ticket | belit | بلیط |
| fare | qeymat-e belit | قیمت بلیط |
| cashier (ticket seller) | sanduqdār | صندوقدار |
| ticket inspection | kontorol-e belit | کنترل بلیط |
| ticket inspector | kontorol či | کنترل چی |

| to be late (for ...) | ta'xir dāštan | تأخیرداشتن |
| to miss (~ the train, etc.) | az dast dādan | از دست دادن |
| to be in a hurry | ajale kardan | عجله کردن |

| taxi, cab | tāksi | تاکسی |
| taxi driver | rānande-ye tāksi | راننده تاکسی |
| by taxi | bā tāksi | با تاکسی |
| taxi stand | istgāh-e tāksi | ایستگاه تاکسی |
| to call a taxi | tāksi gereftan | تاکسی گرفتن |
| to take a taxi | tāksi gereftan | تاکسی گرفتن |

| traffic | obur-o morur | عبور و مرور |
| traffic jam | terāfik | ترافیک |
| rush hour | sā'at-e šoluqi | ساعت شلوغی |
| to park (vi) | pārk kardan | پارک کردن |
| to park (vt) | pārk kardan | پارک کردن |
| parking lot | pārking | پارکینگ |

| subway | metro | مترو |
| station | istgāh | ایستگاه |
| to take the subway | bā metro raftan | با مترو رفتن |
| train | qatār | قطار |
| train station | istgāh-e rāh-e āhan | ایستگاه راه آهن |

## 57. Sightseeing

| | | |
|---|---|---|
| monument | mojassame | مجسمه |
| fortress | qal'e | قلعه |
| palace | kāx | کاخ |
| castle | qal'e | قلعه |
| tower | borj | برج |
| mausoleum | ārāmgāh | آرامگاه |

| | | |
|---|---|---|
| architecture | me'māri | معماری |
| medieval (adj) | qorun-e vasati | قرون وسطی |
| ancient (adj) | qadimi | قدیمی |
| national (adj) | melli | ملی |
| famous (monument, etc.) | mašhur | مشهور |

| | | |
|---|---|---|
| tourist | turist | توریست |
| guide (person) | rāhnamā-ye tur | راهنمای تور |
| excursion, sightseeing tour | gardeš | گردش |
| to show (vt) | nešān dādan | نشان دادن |
| to tell (vt) | hekāyat kardan | حکایت کردن |

| | | |
|---|---|---|
| to find (vt) | peydā kardan | پیدا کردن |
| to get lost (lose one's way) | gom šodan | گم شدن |
| map (e.g., subway ~) | naqše | نقشه |
| map (e.g., city ~) | naqše | نقشه |

| | | |
|---|---|---|
| souvenir, gift | sowqāti | سوغاتی |
| gift shop | forušgāh-e sowqāti | فروشگاه سوغاتی |
| to take pictures | aks gereftan | عکس گرفتن |
| to have one's picture taken | aks gereftan | عکس گرفتن |

## 58. Shopping

| | | |
|---|---|---|
| to buy (purchase) | xarid kardan | خرید کردن |
| purchase | xarid | خرید |
| to go shopping | xarid kardan | خرید کردن |
| shopping | xarid | خرید |

| | | |
|---|---|---|
| to be open (ab. store) | bāz budan | باز بودن |
| to be closed | baste budan | بسته بودن |

| | | |
|---|---|---|
| footwear, shoes | kafš | کفش |
| clothes, clothing | lebās | لباس |
| cosmetics | lavāzem-e ārāyeši | لوازم آرایشی |
| food products | mavādd-e qazāyi | مواد غذایی |
| gift, present | hedye | هدیه |

| | | |
|---|---|---|
| salesman | forušande | فروشنده |
| saleswoman | forušande-ye zan | فروشنده زن |

| check out, cash desk | sanduq | صندوق |
| mirror | āyene | آینه |
| counter (store ~) | pišxān | پیشخوان |
| fitting room | otāq porov | اتاق پرو |

| to try on | emtehān kardan | امتحان کردن |
| to fit (ab. dress, etc.) | monāseb budan | مناسب بودن |
| to like (I like ...) | dust dāštan | دوست داشتن |

| price | qeymat | قیمت |
| price tag | barčasb-e qeymat | برچسب قیمت |
| to cost (vt) | qeymat dāštan | قیمت داشتن |
| How much? | čeqadr? | چقدر؟ |
| discount | taxfif | تخفیف |

| inexpensive (adj) | arzān | ارزان |
| cheap (adj) | arzān | ارزان |
| expensive (adj) | gerān | گران |
| It's expensive | gerān ast | گران است |

| rental (n) | kerāye | کرایه |
| to rent (~ a tuxedo) | kerāye kardan | کرایه کردن |
| credit (trade credit) | vām | وام |
| on credit (adv) | xarid-e e'tebāri | خرید اعتباری |

## 59. Money

| money | pul | پول |
| currency exchange | tabdil-e arz | تبدیل ارز |
| exchange rate | nerx-e arz | نرخ ارز |
| ATM | xodpardāz | خودپرداز |
| coin | sekke | سکه |

| dollar | dolār | دلار |
| euro | yuro | یورو |

| lira | lire | لیره |
| Deutschmark | mārk | مارک |
| franc | farānak | فرانک |
| pound sterling | pond-e esterling | پوند استرلینگ |
| yen | yen | ین |

| debt | qarz | قرض |
| debtor | bedehkār | بدهکار |
| to lend (money) | qarz dādan | قرض دادن |
| to borrow (vi, vt) | qarz gereftan | قرض گرفتن |

| bank | bānk | بانک |
| account | hesāb-e bānki | حساب بانکی |
| to deposit (vt) | rixtan | ریختن |

| | | |
|---|---|---|
| to deposit into the account | be hesāb rixtan | به حساب ریختن |
| to withdraw (vt) | az hesāb bardāštan | از حساب برداشتن |
| credit card | kārt-e e'tebāri | کارت اعتباری |
| cash | pul-e naqd | پول نقد |
| check | ček | چک |
| to write a check | ček neveštan | چک نوشتن |
| checkbook | daste-ye ček | دسته چک |
| wallet | kif-e pul | کیف پول |
| change purse | kif-e pul | کیف پول |
| safe | gāvsanduq | گاوصندوق |
| heir | vāres | وارث |
| inheritance | mirās | میراث |
| fortune (wealth) | dārāyi | دارایی |
| lease | ejāre | اجاره |
| rent (money) | kerāye-ye xāne | کرایه خانه |
| to rent (sth from sb) | ejāre kardan | اجاره کردن |
| price | qeymat | قیمت |
| cost | arzeš | ارزش |
| sum | jam'-e kol | جمع کل |
| to spend (vt) | xarj kardan | خرج کردن |
| expenses | maxārej | مخارج |
| to economize (vi, vt) | sarfeju-yi kardan | صرفه جویی کردن |
| economical | maqrun besarfe | مقرون به صرفه |
| to pay (vi, vt) | pardāxtan | پرداختن |
| payment | pardāxt | پرداخت |
| change (give the ~) | pul-e xerad | پول خرد |
| tax | māliyāt | مالیات |
| fine | jarime | جریمه |
| to fine (vt) | jarime kardan | جریمه کردن |

## 60. Post. Postal service

| | | |
|---|---|---|
| post office | post | پست |
| mail (letters, etc.) | post | پست |
| mailman | nāme resān | نامه رسان |
| opening hours | sā'athā-ye kāri | ساعت های کاری |
| letter | nāme | نامه |
| registered letter | nāme-ye sefāreši | نامه سفارشی |
| postcard | kārt-e postāl | کارت پستال |
| telegram | telegrām | تلگرام |
| package (parcel) | baste posti | بسته پستی |

|  |  |  |
|---|---|---|
| money transfer | havāle | حواله |
| to receive (vt) | gereftan | گرفتن |
| to send (vt) | ferestādan | فرستادن |
| sending | ersāl | ارسال |
| | | |
| address | nešāni | نشانی |
| ZIP code | kod-e posti | کد پستی |
| sender | ferestande | فرستنده |
| receiver | girande | گیرنده |
| | | |
| name (first name) | esm | اسم |
| surname (last name) | nām-e xānevādegi | نام خانوادگی |
| | | |
| postage rate | ta'refe | تعرفه |
| standard (adj) | ādi | عادی |
| economical (adj) | ādi | عادی |
| | | |
| weight | vazn | وزن |
| to weigh (~ letters) | vazn kardan | وزن کردن |
| envelope | pākat | پاکت |
| postage stamp | tambr | تمبر |
| to stamp an envelope | tamr zadan | تمبر زدن |

# Dwelling. House. Home

## 61. House. Electricity

| electricity | barq | برق |
| light bulb | lāmp | لامپ |

| switch | kelid | کلید |
| fuse (plug fuse) | fiyuz | فیوز |

| cable, wire (electric ~) | sim | سیم |
| wiring | sim keši | سیم کشی |

| electricity meter | kontor | کنتور |
| readings | dastgāh-e xaneš | دستگاه خوانش |

## 62. Villa. Mansion

| country house | xāne-ye xārej-e šahr | خانۀ خارج شهر |
| villa (seaside ~) | vilā | ویلا |
| wing (~ of a building) | bāl | بال |

| garden | bāq | باغ |
| park | pārk | پارک |

| tropical greenhouse | golxāne | گلخانه |
| to look after (garden, etc.) | negahdāri kardan | نگهداری کردن |

| swimming pool | estaxr | استخر |
| gym (home gym) | sālon-e varzeš | سالن ورزش |
| tennis court | zamin-e tenis | زمین تنیس |

| home theater (room) | sinamā | سینما |
| garage | gārāž | گاراژ |

| private property | melk-e xosusi | ملک خصوصی |
| private land | melk-e xosusi | ملک خصوصی |

| warning (caution) | hošdār | هشدار |
| warning sign | alāmat-e hošdār | علامت هشدار |

| security | hefāzat | حفاظت |
| security guard | negahbān | نگهبان |
| burglar alarm | dozdgir | دزدگیر |

## 63. Apartment

| | | |
|---|---|---|
| apartment | āpārtemān | آپارتمان |
| room | otāq | اتاق |
| bedroom | otāq-e xāb | اتاق خواب |
| dining room | otāq-e qazāxori | اتاق غذاخوری |
| living room | mehmānxāne | مهمانخانه |
| study (home office) | daftar | دفتر |
| entry room | tālār-e vorudi | تالار ورودی |
| bathroom (room with a bath or shower) | hammām | حمام |
| half bath | tuālet | توالت |
| ceiling | saqf | سقف |
| floor | kaf | کف |
| corner | guše | گوشه |

## 64. Furniture. Interior

| | | |
|---|---|---|
| furniture | mobl | مبل |
| table | miz | میز |
| chair | sandali | صندلی |
| bed | taxt-e xāb | تخت خواب |
| couch, sofa | kānāpe | کاناپه |
| armchair | mobl-e rāhati | مبل راحتی |
| bookcase | qafase-ye ketāb | قفسه کتاب |
| shelf | qafase | قفسه |
| wardrobe | komod | کمد |
| coat rack (wall-mounted ~) | raxt āviz | رخت آویز |
| coat stand | čub lebāsi | چوب لباسی |
| bureau, dresser | komod | کمد |
| coffee table | miz-e pišdasti | میز پیشدستی |
| mirror | āyene | آینه |
| carpet | farš | فرش |
| rug, small carpet | qāliče | قالیچه |
| fireplace | šumine | شومینه |
| candle | šam' | شمع |
| candlestick | šam'dān | شمعدان |
| drapes | parde | پرده |
| wallpaper | kāqaz-e divāri | کاغذ دیواری |
| blinds (jalousie) | kerkere | کرکره |
| table lamp | čerāq-e rumizi | چراغ رومیزی |

| wall lamp (sconce) | čerāq-e divāri | چراغ دیواری |
| floor lamp | ābāžur | آباژور |
| chandelier | luster | لوستر |

| leg (of chair, table) | pāye | پایه |
| armrest | daste-ye sandali | دستۀ صندلی |
| back (backrest) | pošti | پشتی |
| drawer | kešow | کشو |

## 65. Bedding

| bedclothes | raxt-e xāb | رخت خواب |
| pillow | bālešt | بالشت |
| pillowcase | rubalešt | روبالشت |
| duvet, comforter | patu | پتو |
| sheet | malāfe | ملافه |
| bedspread | rutaxti | روتختی |

## 66. Kitchen

| kitchen | āšpazxāne | آشپزخانه |
| gas | gāz | گاز |
| gas stove (range) | ojāgh-e gāz | اجاق گاز |
| electric stove | ojāgh-e barghi | اجاق برقی |
| oven | fer | فر |
| microwave oven | māykrofer | مایکروفر |

| refrigerator | yaxčāl | یخچال |
| freezer | fereyzer | فریزر |
| dishwasher | māšin-e zarfšuyi | ماشین ظرفشویی |

| meat grinder | čarx-e gušt | چرخ گوشت |
| juicer | ābmive giri | آبمیوه گیری |
| toaster | towster | توستر |
| mixer | maxlut kon | مخلوط کن |

| coffee machine | qahve sāz | قهوه ساز |
| coffee pot | qahve juš | قهوه جوش |
| coffee grinder | āsiyāb-e qahve | آسیاب قهوه |

| kettle | ketri | کتری |
| teapot | quri | قوری |
| lid | sarpuš | سرپوش |
| tea strainer | čāy sāf kon | چای صاف کن |

| spoon | qāšoq | قاشق |
| teaspoon | qāšoq čāy xori | قاشق چای خوری |
| soup spoon | qāšoq sup xori | قاشق سوپ خوری |

| fork | čangāl | چنگال |
| knife | kārd | کارد |

| tableware (dishes) | zoruf | ظروف |
| plate (dinner ~) | bošqāb | بشقاب |
| saucer | na'lbeki | نعلبکی |

| shot glass | gilās-e vodkā | گیلاس ودکا |
| glass (tumbler) | estekān | استکان |
| cup | fenjān | فنجان |

| sugar bowl | qandān | قندان |
| salt shaker | namakdān | نمکدان |
| pepper shaker | felfeldān | فلفلدان |
| butter dish | zarf-e kare | ظرف کره |

| stock pot (soup pot) | qāblame | قابلمه |
| frying pan (skillet) | tābe | تابه |
| ladle | malāqe | ملاقه |
| colander | ābkeš | آبکش |
| tray (serving ~) | sini | سینی |

| bottle | botri | بطری |
| jar (glass) | šiše | شیشه |
| can | quti | قوطی |

| bottle opener | dar bāz kon | در بازکن |
| can opener | dar bāz kon | در بازکن |
| corkscrew | dar bāz kon | در بازکن |
| filter | filter | فیلتر |
| to filter (vt) | filter kardan | فیلتر کردن |

| trash, garbage (food waste, etc.) | āšqāl | آشغال |
| trash can (kitchen ~) | satl-e zobāle | سطل زباله |

## 67. Bathroom

| bathroom | hammām | حمام |
| water | āb | آب |
| faucet | šir | شیر |
| hot water | āb-e dāq | آب داغ |
| cold water | āb-e sard | آب سرد |

| toothpaste | xamir-e dandān | خمیر دندان |
| to brush one's teeth | mesvāk zadan | مسواک زدن |
| toothbrush | mesvāk | مسواک |

| to shave (vi) | riš tarāšidan | ریش تراشیدن |
| shaving foam | xamir-e eslāh | خمیر اصلاح |

| | | |
|---|---|---|
| razor | tiq | تیغ |
| to wash (one's hands, etc.) | šostan | شستن |
| to take a bath | hamām kardan | حمام کردن |
| shower | duš | دوش |
| to take a shower | duš gereftan | دوش گرفتن |
| bathtub | vān hammām | وان حمام |
| toilet (toilet bowl) | tuālet-e farangi | توالت فرنگی |
| sink (washbasin) | sink | سینک |
| soap | sābun | صابون |
| soap dish | jā sābun | جا صابون |
| sponge | abr | ابر |
| shampoo | šāmpu | شامپو |
| towel | howle | حوله |
| bathrobe | howle-ye hamām | حوله حمام |
| laundry (process) | raxčuyi | لباسشویی |
| washing machine | māšin-e lebas-šui | ماشین لباسشویی |
| to do the laundry | šostan-e lebās | شستن لباس |
| laundry detergent | pudr-e lebas-šui | پودر لباسشویی |

## 68. Household appliances

| | | |
|---|---|---|
| TV set | televiziyon | تلویزیون |
| tape recorder | zabt-e sowt | ضبط صوت |
| VCR (video recorder) | video | ویدئو |
| radio | rādiyo | رادیو |
| player (CD, MP3, etc.) | paxš konande | پخش کننده |
| video projector | video porožektor | ویدئو پروژکتور |
| home movie theater | sinamā-ye xānegi | سینمای خانگی |
| DVD player | paxš konande-ye di vi di | پخش کننده دی وی دی |
| amplifier | āmpli-fāyer | آمپلی فایر |
| video game console | konsul-e bāzi | کنسول بازی |
| video camera | durbin-e filmbardāri | دوربین فیلمبرداری |
| camera (photo) | durbin-e akkāsi | دوربین عکاسی |
| digital camera | durbin-e dijitāl | دوربین دیجیتال |
| vacuum cleaner | jāru barqi | جارو برقی |
| iron (e.g., steam ~) | oto | اتو |
| ironing board | miz-e otu | میز اتو |
| telephone | telefon | تلفن |
| cell phone | telefon-e hamrāh | تلفن همراه |
| typewriter | māšin-e tahrir | ماشین تحریر |
| sewing machine | čarx-e xayyāti | چرخ خیاطی |
| microphone | mikrofon | میکروفون |

| | | |
|---|---|---|
| headphones | guši | گوشی |
| remote control (TV) | kontorol az rāh-e dur | کنترل از راه دور |
| | | |
| CD, compact disc | si-di | سیدی |
| cassette, tape | kāst | کاست |
| vinyl record | safhe-ye gerāmāfon | صفحه گرامافون |

# HUMAN ACTIVITIES

## Job. Business. Part 1

### 69. Office. Working in the office

| | | |
|---|---|---|
| office (company ~) | daftar | دفتر |
| office (of director, etc.) | daftar | دفتر |
| reception desk | pazir-aš | پذیرش |
| secretary | monši | منشی |
| secretary (fem.) | monši | منشی |
| | | |
| director | modir | مدیر |
| manager | modir | مدیر |
| accountant | hesābdār | حسابدار |
| employee | kārmand | کارمند |
| | | |
| furniture | mobl | مبل |
| desk | miz | میز |
| desk chair | sandali dastedār | صندلی دسته دار |
| drawer unit | kešow | کشو |
| coat stand | čub lebāsi | چوب لباسی |
| | | |
| computer | kāmpiyuter | کامپیوتر |
| printer | pirinter | پرینتر |
| fax machine | faks | فکس |
| photocopier | dastgāh-e kopi | دستگاه کپی |
| | | |
| paper | kāqaz | کاغذ |
| office supplies | lavāzem-e tahrir | لوازم تحریر |
| mouse pad | māows pad | ماوس پد |
| sheet (of paper) | varaq | ورق |
| binder | puše | پوشه |
| | | |
| catalog | kātālog | کاتالوگ |
| phone directory | rāhnamā | راهنما |
| documentation | asnād | اسناد |
| brochure<br>(e.g., 12 pages ~) | borušur | بروشور |
| | | |
| leaflet (promotional ~) | borušur | بروشور |
| sample | nemune | نمونه |
| | | |
| training meeting | āmuzeš | آموزش |
| meeting (of managers) | jalase | جلسه |
| lunch time | vaqt-e nāhār | وقت ناهار |

| to make a copy | kopi gereftan | کپی گرفتن |
| to make multiple copies | kopi gereftan | کپی گرفتن |
| to receive a fax | faks gereftan | فکس گرفتن |
| to send a fax | faks ferestādan | فکس فرستادن |

| to call (by phone) | telefon zadan | تلفن زدن |
| to answer (vt) | javāb dādan | جواب دادن |
| to put through | vasl šodan | وصل شدن |

| to arrange, to set up | sāzmān dādan | سازمان دادن |
| to demonstrate (vt) | nemāyeš dādan | نمایش دادن |
| to be absent | qāyeb budan | غایب بودن |
| absence | qeybat | غیبت |

## 70. Business processes. Part 1

| occupation | šoql | شغل |
| firm | šerkat | شرکت |
| company | kompāni | کمپانی |
| corporation | šerkat-e sahami | شرکت سهامی |
| enterprise | šerkat | شرکت |
| agency | namāyandegi | نمایندگی |

| agreement (contract) | qarārdād | قرارداد |
| contract | qarārdād | قرارداد |
| deal | mo'āmele | معامله |
| order (to place an ~) | sefāreš | سفارش |
| terms (of the contract) | šart | شرط |

| wholesale (adv) | omde furuši | عمده فروشی |
| wholesale (adj) | omde | عمده |
| wholesale (n) | omde furuši | عمده فروشی |
| retail (adj) | xorde-foruši | خرده فروشی |
| retail (n) | xorde-foruši | خرده فروشی |

| competitor | raqib | رقیب |
| competition | reqābat | رقابت |
| to compete (vi) | reqābat kardan | رقابت کردن |

| partner (associate) | šarik | شریک |
| partnership | mošārek-at | مشارکت |

| crisis | bohrān | بحران |
| bankruptcy | varšekastegi | ورشکستگی |
| to go bankrupt | varšekast šodan | ورشکست شدن |
| difficulty | saxti | سختی |
| problem | moškel | مشکل |
| catastrophe | fāje'e | فاجعه |
| economy | eqtesād | اقتصاد |
| economic (~ growth) | eqtesādi | اقتصادی |

| economic recession | rokud-e eqtesādi | رکود اقتصادی |
| goal (aim) | hadaf | هدف |
| task | hadaf | هدف |

| to trade (vi) | tejārat kardan | تجارت کردن |
| network (distribution ~) | šabake-ye towzi' | شبکهٔ توزیع |
| inventory (stock) | fehrest anbār | فهرست انبار |
| range (assortment) | majmu'e | مجموعه |

| leader (leading company) | rahbar | رهبر |
| large (~ company) | bozorg | بزرگ |
| monopoly | enhesār | انحصار |

| theory | nazariye | نظریه |
| practice | amal | عمل |
| experience (in my ~) | tajrobe | تجربه |
| trend (tendency) | gerāyeš | گرایش |
| development | pišraft | پیشرفت |

## 71. Business processes. Part 2

| profit (foregone ~) | sud | سود |
| profitable (~ deal) | sudāvar | سودآور |

| delegation (group) | hey'at-e namāyandegān | هیئت نمایندگان |
| salary | hoquq | حقوق |
| to correct (an error) | eslāh kardan | اصلاح کردن |
| business trip | ma'muriyat | مأموریت |
| commission | komisiyon | کمیسیون |

| to control (vt) | kontorol kardan | کنترل کردن |
| conference | konferāns | کنفرانس |
| license | parvāne | پروانه |
| reliable (~ partner) | motmaen | مطمئن |

| initiative (undertaking) | ebtekār | ابتکار |
| norm (standard) | me'yār | معیار |
| circumstance | vaz'iyat | وضعیت |
| duty (of employee) | vazife | وظیفه |

| organization (company) | šerkat | شرکت |
| organization (process) | sāzmāndehi | سازماندهی |
| organized (adj) | sāzmān yāfte | سازمان یافته |
| cancellation | laqv | لغو |
| to cancel (call off) | laqv kardan | لغو کردن |
| report (official ~) | gozāreš | گزارش |

| patent | govāhi-ye sabt-e exterā' | گواهی ثبت اختراع |
| to patent (obtain patent) | govāhi exterā' gereftan | گواهی اختراع گرفتن |
| to plan (vt) | barnāmerizi kardan | برنامه ریزی کردن |

| bonus (money) | pādāš | پاداش |
| professional (adj) | herfe i | حرفه ای |
| procedure | tašrifāt | تشریفات |

| to examine (contract, etc.) | barresi kardan | بررسی کردن |
| calculation | mohāsebe | محاسبه |
| reputation | e'tebār | اعتبار |
| risk | risk | ریسک |

| to manage, to run | edāre kardan | اداره کردن |
| information | ettelā'āt | اطلاعات |
| property | dārāyi | دارایی |
| union | ettehādiye | اتحادیه |

| life insurance | bime-ye omr | بیمهٔ عمر |
| to insure (vt) | bime kardan | بیمه کردن |
| insurance | bime | بیمه |

| auction (~ sale) | harāj | حراج |
| to notify (inform) | xabar dādan | خبر دادن |
| management (process) | edāre | اداره |
| service (~ industry) | xedmat | خدمت |

| forum | ham andiši | هم اندیشی |
| to function (vi) | amal kardan | عمل کردن |
| stage (phase) | marhale | مرحله |
| legal (~ services) | hoquqi | حقوقی |
| lawyer (legal advisor) | hoquq dān | حقوق دان |

## 72. Production. Works

| plant | kārxāne | کارخانه |
| factory | kārxāne | کارخانه |
| workshop | kārgāh | کارگاه |
| works, production site | towlidi | تولیدی |

| industry (manufacturing) | san'at | صنعت |
| industrial (adj) | san'ati | صنعتی |
| heavy industry | sanāye-'e sangin | صنایع سنگین |
| light industry | sanāye-'e sabok | صنایع سبک |

| products | towlidāt | تولیدات |
| to produce (vt) | towlid kardan | تولید کردن |
| raw materials | mavādd-e xām | مواد خام |

| foreman (construction ~) | sarkāregar | سرکارگر |
| workers team (crew) | daste-ye kāregaran | دسته کارگران |
| worker | kārgar | کارگر |
| working day | ruz-e kāri | روز کاری |
| pause (rest break) | esterāhat | استراحت |

| meeting | jalase | جلسه |
|---|---|---|
| to discuss (vt) | bahs kardan | بحث کردن |

| plan | barnāme | برنامه |
|---|---|---|
| to fulfill the plan | barnāme rā ejrā kardan | برنامه را اجرا کردن |
| rate of output | nerx-e tolid | نرخ تولید |
| quality | keyfiyat | کیفیت |
| control (checking) | kontorol | کنترل |
| quality control | kontorol-e keyfi | کنترل کیفی |

| workplace safety | amniyat-e kār | امنیت کار |
|---|---|---|
| discipline | enzebāt | انضباط |
| violation | naqz | نقض |
| (of safety rules, etc.) | | |
| to violate (rules) | naqz kardan | نقض کردن |

| strike | e'tesāb | اعتصاب |
|---|---|---|
| striker | e'tesāb konande | اعتصاب کننده |

| to be on strike | e'tesāb kardan | اعتصاب کردن |
|---|---|---|
| labor union | ettehādiye-ye kārgari | اتحادیۀ کارگری |

| to invent (machine, etc.) | exterā' kardan | اختراع کردن |
|---|---|---|
| invention | exterā' | اختراع |
| research | tahqiq | تحقیق |
| to improve (make better) | behtar kardan | بهتر کردن |

| technology | fanāvari | فناوری |
|---|---|---|
| technical drawing | rasm-e fani | رسم فنی |

| load, cargo | bār | بار |
|---|---|---|
| loader (person) | bārbar | باربر |
| to load (vehicle, etc.) | bār kardan | بار کردن |
| loading (process) | bārgiri | بارگیری |

| to unload (vi, vt) | bārgiri | بارگیری |
|---|---|---|
| unloading | bārandāz-i | باراندازی |

| transportation | haml-o naql | حمل و نقل |
|---|---|---|
| transportation company | šerkat-e haml-o naql | شرکت حمل و نقل |
| to transport (vt) | haml kardan | حمل کردن |

| freight car | vāgon-e bari | واگن باری |
|---|---|---|
| tank (e.g., oil ~) | maxzan | مخزن |
| truck | kāmiyon | کامیون |

| machine tool | dastgāh | دستگاه |
|---|---|---|
| mechanism | mekānism | مکانیسم |

| industrial waste | zāye'āt-e san'ati | ضایعات صنعتی |
|---|---|---|
| packing (process) | baste band-i | بسته بندی |
| to pack (vt) | baste bandi kardan | بسته بندی کردن |

## 73. Contract. Agreement

| | | |
|---|---|---|
| contract | qarārdād | قرارداد |
| agreement | tavāfoq-e nāme | توافق نامه |
| addendum | zamime | ضمیمه |
| | | |
| to sign a contract | qarārdād bastan | قرارداد بستن |
| signature | emzā' | امضاء |
| to sign (vt) | emzā kardan | امضا کردن |
| seal (stamp) | mehr | مهر |
| | | |
| subject of contract | mowzu-'e qarārdād | موضوع قرارداد |
| clause | mādde | ماده |
| parties (in contract) | tarafeyn | طرفین |
| legal address | ādres-e hoquqi | آدرس حقوقی |
| | | |
| to violate the contract | naqz kardan-e qarārdād | نقض کردن قرارداد |
| commitment (obligation) | ta'ahhod | تعهد |
| responsibility | mas'uliyat | مسئولیت |
| force majeure | šarāyet-e ezterāri | شرایط اضطراری |
| dispute | xalāf | خلاف |
| penalties | eqdāmāt-e tanbihi | اقدامات تنبیهی |

## 74. Import & Export

| | | |
|---|---|---|
| import | vāredāt | واردات |
| importer | vāred konande | وارد کننده |
| to import (vt) | vāred kardan | وارد کردن |
| import (as adj.) | vāredāti | وارداتی |
| | | |
| export (exportation) | sāderāt | صادرات |
| exporter | sāder konande | صادر کننده |
| to export (vi, vt) | sāder kardan | صادر کردن |
| export (as adj.) | sāderāti | صادراتی |
| | | |
| goods (merchandise) | kālā | کالا |
| consignment, lot | mahmule | محموله |
| | | |
| weight | vazn | وزن |
| volume | hajm | حجم |
| cubic meter | metr moka'ab | متر مکعب |
| | | |
| manufacturer | towlid konande | تولید کننده |
| transportation company | šerkat-e haml-o naql | شرکت حمل و نقل |
| container | kāntiner | کانتینر |
| | | |
| border | marz | مرز |
| customs | gomrok | گمرک |
| customs duty | avārez-e gomroki | عوارض گمرکی |

| | | |
|---|---|---|
| customs officer | ma'mur-e gomrok | مأمور گمرک |
| smuggling | qāčāq | قاچاق |
| contraband (smuggled goods) | ajnās-e qāčāq | اجناس قاچاق |

## 75. Finances

| | | |
|---|---|---|
| stock (share) | sahām | سهام |
| bond (certificate) | owrāq-e bahādār | اوراق بهادار |
| promissory note | safte | سفته |
| | | |
| stock exchange | burs | بورس |
| stock price | nerx-e sahām | نرخ سهام |
| | | |
| to go down (become cheaper) | arzān šodan | ارزان شدن |
| to go up (become more expensive) | gerān šodan | گران شدن |
| | | |
| controlling interest | manāfe-'e kontoroli | منافع کنترلی |
| investment | sarmāye gozāri | سرمایه گذاری |
| to invest (vt) | sarmāye gozāri kardan | سرمایه گذاری کردن |
| percent | darsad | درصد |
| interest (on investment) | sud | سود |
| | | |
| profit | sud | سود |
| profitable (adj) | sudāvar | سودآور |
| tax | māliyāt | مالیات |
| | | |
| currency (foreign ~) | arz | ارز |
| national (adj) | melli | ملی |
| exchange (currency ~) | tabādol | تبادل |
| | | |
| accountant | hesābdār | حسابدار |
| accounting | hesābdāri | حسابداری |
| | | |
| bankruptcy | varšekastegi | ورشکستگی |
| collapse, crash | šekast | شکست |
| ruin | varšekastegi | ورشکستگی |
| to be ruined (financially) | varšekast šodan | ورشکست شدن |
| inflation | tavarrom | تورم |
| devaluation | taqlil-e arzeš-e pul | تقلیل ارزش پول |
| | | |
| capital | sarmāye | سرمایه |
| income | darāmad | درآمد |
| turnover | gardeš mo'āmelāt | گردش معاملات |
| resources | manābe' | منابع |
| monetary resources | manābe-'e puli | منابع پولی |
| overhead | maxārej-e kolli | مخارج کلی |
| to reduce (expenses) | kam kardan | کم کردن |

## 76. Marketing

| | | |
|---|---|---|
| marketing | bāzāryābi | بازاریابی |
| market | bāzār | بازار |
| market segment | baxše bāzār | بخش بازار |
| product | mahsul | محصول |
| goods (merchandise) | kālā | کالا |
| brand | barand | برند |
| trademark | nešān tejāri | نشان تجاری |
| logotype | logo | لوگو |
| logo | logo | لوگو |
| demand | taqāzā | تقاضا |
| supply | arze | عرضه |
| need | ehtiyāj | احتیاج |
| consumer | masraf-e konande | مصرف کننده |
| analysis | tahlil | تحلیل |
| to analyze (vt) | tahlil kardan | تحلیل کردن |
| positioning | mowze' giri | موضع گیری |
| to position (vt) | mowze' giri kardan | موضع گیری کردن |
| price | qeymat | قیمت |
| pricing policy | siyāsat-e qeymat-e gozār-i | سیاست قیمت گذاری |
| price formation | qeymat gozāri | قیمت گذاری |

## 77. Advertising

| | | |
|---|---|---|
| advertising | āgahi | آگهی |
| to advertise (vt) | tabliq kardan | تبلیغ کردن |
| budget | budje | بودجه |
| ad, advertisement | āgahi | آگهی |
| TV advertising | tabliqāt-e televiziyoni | تبلیغات تلویزیونی |
| radio advertising | tabliqāt-e rādiyoyi | تبلیغات رادیویی |
| outdoor advertising | āgahi-ye biruni | آگهی بیرونی |
| mass media | resāne-hay-e jam'i | رسانه های جمعی |
| periodical (n) | našriye-ye dowrei | نشریۀ دوره ای |
| image (public appearance) | temsāl | تمثال |
| slogan | šo'ār | شعار |
| motto (maxim) | šo'ār | شعار |
| campaign | kampeyn | کمپین |
| advertising campaign | kampeyn-e tabliqāti | کمپین تبلیغاتی |
| target group | goruh-e hadaf | گروه هدف |
| business card | kārt-e vizit | کارت ویزیت |

| leaflet (promotional ~) | borušur | بروشور |
| brochure (e.g., 12 pages ~) | borušur | بروشور |
| pamphlet | ketābče | کتابچه |
| newsletter | xabarnāme | خبرنامه |

| signboard (store sign, etc.) | tāblo | تابلو |
| poster | poster | پوستر |
| billboard | bilbord | بیلبورد |

## 78. Banking

| bank | bānk | بانک |
| branch (of bank, etc.) | šo'be | شعبه |

| bank clerk, consultant | mošāver | مشاور |
| manager (director) | modir | مدیر |

| bank account | hesāb-e bānki | حساب بانکی |
| account number | šomāre-ye hesāb | شمارۀ حساب |
| checking account | hesāb-e jāri | حساب جاری |
| savings account | hesāb-e pasandāz | حساب پس انداز |

| to open an account | hesāb-e bāz kardan | حساب باز کردن |
| to close the account | hesāb rā bastan | حساب را بستن |
| to deposit into the account | be hesāb rixtan | به حساب ریختن |
| to withdraw (vt) | az hesāb bardāštan | از حساب برداشتن |

| deposit | seporde | سپرده |
| to make a deposit | seporde gozāštan | سپرده گذاشتن |
| wire transfer | enteqāl | انتقال |
| to wire, to transfer | enteqāl dādan | انتقال دادن |

| sum | jam'-e kol | جمع کل |
| How much? | čeqadr? | چقدر؟ |

| signature | emzā' | امضاء |
| to sign (vt) | emzā kardan | امضا کردن |

| credit card | kārt-e e'tebāri | کارت اعتباری |
| code (PIN code) | kod | کد |
| credit card number | šomāre-ye kārt-e e'tebāri | شماره کارت اعتباری |
| ATM | xodpardāz | خودپرداز |

| check | ček | چک |
| to write a check | ček neveštan | چک نوشتن |
| checkbook | daste-ye ček | دسته چک |

| loan (bank ~) | e'tebār | اعتبار |
| to apply for a loan | darxāst-e vam kardan | درخواست وام کردن |

| to get a loan | vām gereftan | وام گرفتن |
| to give a loan | vām dādan | وام دادن |
| guarantee | zemānat | ضمانت |

## 79. Telephone. Phone conversation

| telephone | telefon | تلفن |
| cell phone | telefon-e hamrāh | تلفن همراه |
| answering machine | monši-ye telefoni | منشی تلفنی |

| to call (by phone) | telefon zadan | تلفن زدن |
| phone call | tamās-e telefoni | تماس تلفنی |

| to dial a number | šomāre gereftan | شماره گرفتن |
| Hello! | alo! | الو! |
| to ask (vt) | porsidan | پرسیدن |
| to answer (vi, vt) | javāb dādan | جواب دادن |

| to hear (vt) | šenidan | شنیدن |
| well (adv) | xub | خوب |
| not well (adv) | bad | بد |
| noises (interference) | sedā | صدا |

| receiver | guši | گوشی |
| to pick up (~ the phone) | guši rā bar dāštan | گوشی را برداشتن |
| to hang up (~ the phone) | guši rā gozāštan | گوشی را گذاشتن |

| busy (engaged) | mašqul | مشغول |
| to ring (ab. phone) | zang zadan | زنگ زدن |
| telephone book | daftar-e telefon | دفتر تلفن |

| local (adj) | mahalli | محلی |
| local call | telefon-e dāxeli | تلفن داخلی |
| long distance (~ call) | beyn-e šahri | بین شهری |
| long-distance call | telefon-e beyn-e šahri | تلفن بین شهری |
| international (adj) | beynolmelali | بین المللی |
| international call | telefon-e beynolmelali | تلفن بین المللی |

## 80. Cell phone

| cell phone | telefon-e hamrāh | تلفن همراه |
| display | namāyešgar | نمایشگر |
| button | dokme | دکمه |
| SIM card | sim-e kārt | سیم کارت |

| battery | bātri | باطری |
| to be dead (battery) | tamām šodan bātri | تمام شدن باتری |
| charger | šāržer | شارژ |

| menu | meno | منو |
| settings | tanzimāt | تنظیمات |
| tune (melody) | āhang | آهنگ |
| to select (vt) | entexāb kardan | انتخاب کردن |

| calculator | māšin-e hesāb | ماشین حساب |
| voice mail | monši-ye telefoni | منشی تلفنی |
| alarm clock | sā'at-e zang dār | ساعت زنگ دار |
| contacts | daftar-e telefon | دفتر تلفن |

| SMS (text message) | payāmak | پیامک |
| subscriber | moštarek | مشترک |

## 81. Stationery

| ballpoint pen | xodkār | خودکار |
| fountain pen | xodnevis | خودنویس |

| pencil | medād | مداد |
| highlighter | māžik | ماژیک |
| felt-tip pen | māžik | ماژیک |

| notepad | daftar-e yāddāšt | دفتر یادداشت |
| agenda (diary) | daftar-e yāddāšt | دفتر یادداشت |

| ruler | xat keš | خط کش |
| calculator | māšin-e hesāb | ماشین حساب |
| eraser | pāk kon | پاک کن |
| thumbtack | punez | پونز |
| paper clip | gire | گیره |

| glue | časb | چسب |
| stapler | mangane-ye zan | منگنه زن |
| hole punch | pānč | پانچ |
| pencil sharpener | madād-e tarāš | مداد تراش |

## 82. Kinds of business

| accounting services | xadamāt-e hesābdāri | خدمات حسابداری |
| advertising | āgahi | آگهی |
| advertising agency | āžāns-e tabliqāti | آژانس تبلیغاتی |
| air-conditioners | tahviye-ye matbu' | تهویه مطبوع |
| airline | šerkat-e havāpeymāyi | شرکت هواپیمایی |

| alcoholic beverages | mašrubāt-e alkoli | مشروبات الکلی |
| antiques (antique dealers) | atiqe | عتیقه |
| art gallery (contemporary ~) | gāleri-ye honari | گالری هنری |

| audit services | xadamāt-e momayyezi | خدمات ممیزی |
| banking industry | bānk-dāri | بانکداری |
| bar | bār | بار |
| beauty parlor | sālon-e zibāyi | سالن زیبایی |
| bookstore | ketāb-foruši | کتاب فروشی |
| brewery | ābe jow-sāzi | آب جوسازی |
| business center | markaz-e tejāri | مرکز تجاری |
| business school | moassese-ye bāzargāni | موسسه بازرگانی |
| | | |
| casino | kāzino | کازینو |
| construction | sāxtemān | ساختمان |
| consulting | mošavere | مشاوره |
| | | |
| dental clinic | dandān-e pezeški | دندان پزشکی |
| design | tarrāhi | طراحی |
| drugstore, pharmacy | dāruxāne | داروخانه |
| dry cleaners | xošk-šuyi | خشکشویی |
| employment agency | āžāns-e kāryābi | آژانس کاریابی |
| | | |
| financial services | xadamāt-e māli | خدمات مالی |
| food products | mavādd-e qazāyi | مواد غذایی |
| funeral home | xadamat-e kafno dafn | خدمات کفن ودفن |
| furniture (e.g., house ~) | mobl | مبل |
| clothing, garment | lebās | لباس |
| hotel | hotel | هتل |
| | | |
| ice-cream | bastani | بستنی |
| industry (manufacturing) | san'at | صنعت |
| insurance | bime | بیمه |
| Internet | internet | اینترنت |
| investments (finance) | sarmāye gozāri | سرمایه گذاری |
| | | |
| jeweler | javāheri | جواهری |
| jewelry | javāherāt | جواهرات |
| laundry (shop) | xošk-šuyi | خشکشویی |
| legal advisor | xadamāt-e hoquqi | خدمات حقوقی |
| light industry | sanāye-'e sabok | صنایع سبک |
| | | |
| magazine | majalle | مجله |
| mail-order selling | foruš-e sefāreš-e posti | فروش سفارش پستی |
| medicine | pezeški | پزشکی |
| movie theater | sinamā | سینما |
| museum | muze | موزه |
| | | |
| news agency | xabar-gozari | خبرگزاری |
| newspaper | ruznāme | روزنامه |
| nightclub | kābāre | کاباره |
| | | |
| oil (petroleum) | naft | نفت |
| courier services | xadamāt-e post | خدمات پست |
| pharmaceutics | dārusāzi | داروسازی |
| printing (industry) | sahhāfi | صحافی |

| | | |
|---|---|---|
| publishing house | entešārāt | انتشارات |
| radio (~ station) | rādiyo | رادیو |
| real estate | amvāl-e qeyr-e manqul | اموال غیر منقول |
| restaurant | resturān | رستوران |
| security company | āžāns-e amniyati | آژانس امنیتی |
| sports | varzeš | ورزش |
| stock exchange | burs | بورس |
| store | maqāze | مغازه |
| supermarket | supermārket | سوپرمارکت |
| swimming pool (public ~) | estaxr | استخر |
| tailor shop | xayyāti | خیاطی |
| television | televiziyon | تلویزیون |
| theater | teātr | تئاتر |
| trade (commerce) | tejārat | تجارت |
| transportation | haml-o naql | حمل و نقل |
| travel | turism | توریسم |
| veterinarian | dāmpezešk | دامپزشک |
| warehouse | anbār | انبار |
| waste collection | jam āvari-ye zobāle | جمع آوری زباله |

# Job. Business. Part 2

## 83. Show. Exhibition

|  |  |  |
|---|---|---|
| exhibition, show | namāyešgāh | نمایشگاه |
| trade show | namāyešgāh-e tejāri | نمایشگاه تجاری |
| participation | šerkat | شرکت |
| to participate (vi) | šerekat kardan | شرکت کردن |
| participant (exhibitor) | šerekat konande | شرکت کننده |
| director | ra'is | رئیس |
| organizers' office | daftar-e modiriyat | دفتر مدیریت |
| organizer | sāzmān dahande | سازمان دهنده |
| to organize (vt) | sāzmān dādan | سازمان دادن |
| participation form | darxāst-e šerkat | درخواست شرکت |
| to fill out (vt) | por kardan | پر کردن |
| details | joz'iyāt | جزئیات |
| information | ettelā'āt | اطلاعات |
| price (cost, rate) | arzeš | ارزش |
| including | šāmel | شامل |
| to include (vt) | šāmel šodan | شامل شدن |
| to pay (vi, vt) | pardāxtan | پرداختن |
| registration fee | haqq-e sabt | حق ثبت |
| entrance | vorud | ورود |
| pavilion, hall | qorfe | غرفه |
| to register (vt) | sabt kardan | ثبت کردن |
| badge (identity tag) | kārt-e šenāsāyi | کارت شناسایی |
| booth, stand | qorfe | غرفه |
| to reserve, to book | rezerv kardan | رزرو کردن |
| display case | vitrin | ویترین |
| spotlight | nurafkan | نورافکن |
| design | tarh | طرح |
| to place (put, set) | qarār dādan | قرار دادن |
| to be placed | qarār gereftan | قرار گرفتن |
| distributor | towzi' konande | توزیع کننده |
| supplier | arze konande | عرضه کننده |
| to supply (vt) | arze kardan | عرضه کردن |
| country | kešvar | کشور |
| foreign (adj) | xāreji | خارجی |

| | | |
|---|---|---|
| product | mahsul | محصول |
| association | anjoman | انجمن |
| conference hall | tālār-e konferāns | تالار کنفرانس |
| congress | kongere | کنگره |
| contest (competition) | mosābeqe | مسابقه |

| | | |
|---|---|---|
| visitor (attendee) | bāzdid konande | بازدید کننده |
| to visit (attend) | bāzdid kardan | بازدید کردن |
| customer | moštari | مشتری |

## 84. Science. Research. Scientists

| | | |
|---|---|---|
| science | elm | علم |
| scientific (adj) | elmi | علمی |
| scientist | dānešmand | دانشمند |
| theory | nazariye | نظریه |

| | | |
|---|---|---|
| axiom | qā'ede-ye kolli | قاعده کلی |
| analysis | tahlil | تحلیل |
| to analyze (vt) | tahlil kardan | تحلیل کردن |
| argument (strong ~) | dalil | دلیل |
| substance (matter) | mādde | ماده |

| | | |
|---|---|---|
| hypothesis | farziye | فرضیه |
| dilemma | dorāhi | دوراهی |
| dissertation | pāyān nāme | پایان نامه |
| dogma | aqide | عقیده |

| | | |
|---|---|---|
| doctrine | doktorin | دکترین |
| research | tahqiq | تحقیق |
| to research (vt) | tahghigh kardan | تحقیق کردن |
| tests (laboratory ~) | āzmāyeš | آزمایش |
| laboratory | āzmāyešgāh | آزمایشگاه |

| | | |
|---|---|---|
| method | raveš | روش |
| molecule | molekul | مولکول |
| monitoring | nozzār-at | نظارت |
| discovery (act, event) | kašf | کشف |

| | | |
|---|---|---|
| postulate | engāre | انگاره |
| principle | asl | اصل |
| forecast | piš bini | پیش بینی |
| to forecast (vt) | pišbini kardan | پیش بینی کردن |

| | | |
|---|---|---|
| synthesis | santez | سنتز |
| trend (tendency) | gerāyeš | گرایش |
| theorem | qaziye | قضیه |

| | | |
|---|---|---|
| teachings | āmuzeš | آموزش |
| fact | haqiqat | حقیقت |

| | | |
|---|---|---|
| expedition | safar | سفر |
| experiment | āzmāyeš | آزمایش |
| | | |
| academician | ozv-e ākādemi | عضو آکادمی |
| bachelor (e.g., ~ of Arts) | lisāns | لیسانس |
| doctor (PhD) | pezešk | پزشک |
| Associate Professor | dānešyār | دانشیار |
| Master (e.g., ~ of Arts) | foqe lisāns | فوق لیسانس |
| professor | porofosor | پروفسور |

# Professions and occupations

## 85. Job search. Dismissal

| job | kār | کار |
| staff (work force) | kārmandān | کارمندان |
| personnel | kādr | کادر |

| career | šoql | شغل |
| prospects (chances) | durnamā | دورنما |
| skills (mastery) | mahārat | مهارت |

| selection (screening) | entexāb | انتخاب |
| employment agency | āžāns-e kāryābi | آژانس کاریابی |
| résumé | rezume | رزومه |
| job interview | mosāhabe-ye kari | مصاحبه کاری |
| vacancy, opening | post-e xāli | پست خالی |

| salary, pay | hoquq | حقوق |
| fixed salary | darāmad-e s ābet | درآمد ثابت |
| pay, compensation | pardāxt | پرداخت |

| position (job) | šoql | شغل |
| duty (of employee) | vazife | وظیفه |
| range of duties | šarh-e vazāyef | شرح وظایف |
| busy (I'm ~) | mašqul | مشغول |

| to fire (dismiss) | exrāj kardan | اخراج کردن |
| dismissal | exrāj | اخراج |

| unemployment | bikāri | بیکاری |
| unemployed (n) | bikār | بیکار |
| retirement | mostamerri | مستمری |
| to retire (from job) | bāznešaste šodan | بازنشسته شدن |

## 86. Business people

| director | modir | مدیر |
| manager (director) | modir | مدیر |
| boss | ra'is | رئیس |

| superior | māfowq | مافوق |
| superiors | roasā | رؤسا |
| president | ra'is jomhur | رئیس جمهور |

| chairman | ra'is | رئیس |
|---|---|---|
| deputy (substitute) | mo'āven | معاون |
| assistant | mo'āven | معاون |
| secretary | monši | منشی |
| personal assistant | dastyār-e šaxsi | دستیار شخصی |

| businessman | bāzargān | بازرگان |
|---|---|---|
| entrepreneur | kārāfarin | کارآفرین |
| founder | moasses | مؤسس |
| to found (vt) | ta'sis kardan | تأسیس کردن |

| incorporator | hamkār | همکار |
|---|---|---|
| partner | šarik | شریک |
| stockholder | sahāmdār | سهامدار |

| millionaire | milyuner | میلیونر |
|---|---|---|
| billionaire | milyārder | میلیاردر |
| owner, proprietor | sāheb | صاحب |
| landowner | zamin-dār | زمین دار |

| client | xaridār | خریدار |
|---|---|---|
| regular client | xaridār-e dāemi | خریدار دائمی |
| buyer (customer) | xaridār | خریدار |
| visitor | bāzdid konande | بازدید کننده |

| professional (n) | herfe i | حرفه ای |
|---|---|---|
| expert | kāršenās | کارشناس |
| specialist | motexasses | متخصص |

| banker | kārmand-e bānk | کارمند بانک |
|---|---|---|
| broker | dallāl-e kārgozār | دلال کارگزار |

| cashier, teller | sanduqdār | صندوقدار |
|---|---|---|
| accountant | hesābdār | حسابدار |
| security guard | negahbān | نگهبان |

| investor | sarmāye gozār | سرمایه گذار |
|---|---|---|
| debtor | bedehkār | بدهکار |
| creditor | talabkār | طلبکار |
| borrower | vām girande | وام گیرنده |

| importer | vāred konande | وارد کننده |
|---|---|---|
| exporter | sāder konande | صادر کننده |

| manufacturer | towlid konande | تولید کننده |
|---|---|---|
| distributor | towzi' konande | توزیع کننده |
| middleman | vāsete | واسطه |

| consultant | mošāver | مشاور |
|---|---|---|
| sales representative | namāyande | نماینده |
| agent | namāyande | نماینده |
| insurance agent | namāyande-ye bime | نمایندۀ بیمه |

## 87. Service professions

| | | |
|---|---|---|
| cook | āšpaz | آشپز |
| chef (kitchen chef) | sarāšpaz | سرآشپز |
| baker | nānvā | نانوا |
| | | |
| bartender | motesaddi-ye bār | متصدی بار |
| waiter | pišxedmat | پیشخدمت |
| waitress | pišxedmat | پیشخدمت |
| | | |
| lawyer, attorney | vakil | وکیل |
| lawyer (legal expert) | hoquq dān | حقوق دان |
| notary | daftardār | دفتردار |
| | | |
| electrician | barq-e kār | برق کار |
| plumber | lule keš | لوله کش |
| carpenter | najjār | نجار |
| | | |
| masseur | māsāž dahande | ماساژ دهنده |
| masseuse | māsāž dahande | ماساژ دهنده |
| doctor | pezešk | پزشک |
| | | |
| taxi driver | rānande-ye tāksi | راننده تاکسی |
| driver | rānande | راننده |
| delivery man | peyk | پیک |
| | | |
| chambermaid | mostaxdem | مستخدم |
| security guard | negahbān | نگهبان |
| flight attendant (fem.) | mehmāndār-e havāpeymā | مهماندار هواپیما |
| | | |
| schoolteacher | mo'allem | معلم |
| librarian | ketābdār | کتابدار |
| translator | motarjem | مترجم |
| interpreter | motarjem-e šafāhi | مترجم شفاهی |
| guide | rāhnamā-ye tur | راهنمای تور |
| | | |
| hairdresser | ārāyešgar | آرایشگر |
| mailman | nāme resān | نامه رسان |
| salesman (store staff) | forušande | فروشنده |
| | | |
| gardener | bāqbān | باغبان |
| domestic servant | nowkar | نوکر |
| maid (female servant) | xedmatkār | خدمتکار |
| cleaner (cleaning lady) | zan-e nezāfatči | زن نظافتچی |

## 88. Military professions and ranks

| | | |
|---|---|---|
| private | sarbāz | سرباز |
| sergeant | goruhbān | گروهبان |

| | | |
|---|---|---|
| lieutenant | sotvān | ستوان |
| captain | kāpitān | کاپیتان |
| | | |
| major | sargord | سرگرد |
| colonel | sarhang | سرهنگ |
| general | ženerāl | ژنرال |
| marshal | māršāl | مارشال |
| admiral | daryāsālār | دریاسالار |
| | | |
| military (n) | nezāmi | نظامی |
| soldier | sarbāz | سرباز |
| officer | afsar | افسر |
| commander | farmāndeh | فرمانده |
| | | |
| border guard | marzbān | مرزبان |
| radio operator | bisim či | بیسیم چی |
| scout (searcher) | ettelā'āti | اطلاعاتی |
| pioneer (sapper) | mohandes estehkāmāt | مهندس استحکامات |
| marksman | tirandāz | تیرانداز |
| navigator | nāvbar | ناویر |

## 89. Officials. Priests

| | | |
|---|---|---|
| king | šāh | شاه |
| queen | maleke | ملکه |
| | | |
| prince | šāhzāde | شاهزاده |
| princess | pranses | پرنسس |
| | | |
| czar | tezār | تزار |
| czarina | maleke | ملکه |
| | | |
| president | ra'is jomhur | رئیس جمهور |
| Secretary (minister) | vazir | وزیر |
| prime minister | noxost vazir | نخست وزیر |
| senator | senātor | سناتور |
| | | |
| diplomat | diplomāt | دیپلمات |
| consul | konsul | کنسول |
| ambassador | safir | سفیر |
| counsilor (diplomatic officer) | mošāver | مشاور |
| | | |
| official, functionary (civil servant) | kārmand | کارمند |
| | | |
| prefect | baxšdār | بخشدار |
| mayor | šahrdār | شهردار |
| judge | qāzi | قاضی |
| prosecutor (e.g., district attorney) | dādsetān | دادستان |

| missionary | misiyoner | میسیونر |
| monk | rāheb | راهب |
| abbot | rāheb-e bozorg | راهب بزرگ |
| rabbi | xāxām | خاخام |

| vizier | vazir | وزیر |
| shah | šāh | شاه |
| sheikh | šeyx | شیخ |

## 90. Agricultural professions

| beekeeper | zanburdār | زنبوردار |
| herder, shepherd | čupān | چوپان |
| agronomist | motexasses-e kešāvarzi | متخصص کشاورزی |
| cattle breeder | dāmparvar | دامپرور |
| veterinarian | dāmpezešk | دامپزشک |

| farmer | kešāvarz | کشاورز |
| winemaker | šarāb sāz | شراب ساز |
| zoologist | jānevar-šenās | جانور شناس |
| cowboy | gāvčerān | گاوچران |

## 91. Art professions

| actor | bāzigar | بازیگر |
| actress | bāzigar | بازیگر |

| singer (masc.) | xānande | خواننده |
| singer (fem.) | xānande | خواننده |

| dancer (masc.) | raqqās | رقاص |
| dancer (fem.) | raqqāse | رقاصه |

| performer (masc.) | honarpiše | هنرپیشه |
| performer (fem.) | honarpiše | هنرپیشه |

| musician | muzisiyan | موزیسین |
| pianist | piyānist | پیانیست |
| guitar player | gitārist | گیتاریست |

| conductor (orchestra ~) | rahbar-e orkestr | رهبر ارکستر |
| composer | āhangsāz | آهنگساز |
| impresario | modir-e operā | مدیر اپرا |

| film director | kārgardān | کارگردان |
| producer | tahiye konande | تهیه کننده |
| scriptwriter | senārist | سناریست |
| critic | montaqed | منتقد |

| writer | nevisande | نویسنده |
| poet | šā'er | شاعر |
| sculptor | mojassame sāz | مجسمه ساز |
| artist (painter) | naqqāš | نقاش |

| juggler | tardast | تردست |
| clown | dalqak | دلقک |
| acrobat | ākrobāt | آکروبات |
| magician | šo'bade bāz | شعبده باز |

## 92. Various professions

| doctor | pezešk | پزشک |
| nurse | parastār | پرستار |
| psychiatrist | ravānpezešk | روانپزشک |
| dentist | dandān pezešk | دندان پزشک |
| surgeon | jarrāh | جراح |

| astronaut | fazānavard | فضانورد |
| astronomer | setāre-šenās | ستاره شناس |
| pilot | xalabān | خلبان |

| driver (of taxi, etc.) | rānande | راننده |
| engineer (train driver) | rānande | راننده |
| mechanic | mekānik | مکانیک |

| miner | ma'dančì | معدنچی |
| worker | kārgar | کارگر |
| locksmith | qofl sāz | قفل ساز |
| joiner (carpenter) | najjār | نجار |
| turner (lathe machine operator) | tarrāš kār | تراش کار |
| construction worker | kārgar-e sāxtemāni | کارگر ساختمانی |
| welder | juš kār | جوش کار |

| professor (title) | porofosor | پروفسور |
| architect | me'mār | معمار |
| historian | movarrex | مورخ |
| scientist | dānešmand | دانشمند |
| physicist | fizikdān | فیزیکدان |
| chemist (scientist) | šimi dān | شیمی دان |

| archeologist | bāstān-šenās | باستان شناس |
| geologist | zamin-šenās | زمین شناس |
| researcher (scientist) | pažuhešgar | پژوهشگر |

| babysitter | parastār bače | پرستار بچه |
| teacher, educator | āmuzgār | آموزگار |
| editor | virāstār | ویراستار |
| editor-in-chief | sardabir | سردبیر |

| correspondent | xabarnegār | خبرنگار |
| typist (fem.) | māšin nevis | ماشین نویس |

| designer | tarāh | طراح |
| computer expert | kāršenās kāmpiyuter | کارشناس کامپیوتر |
| programmer | barnāme-ye nevis | برنامه نویس |
| engineer (designer) | mohandes | مهندس |

| sailor | malavān | ملوان |
| seaman | malavān | ملوان |
| rescuer | nejāt-e dahande | نجات دهنده |

| fireman | ātaš nešān | آتش نشان |
| police officer | polis | پلیس |
| watchman | mohāfez | محافظ |
| detective | kārāgāh | کارآگاه |

| customs officer | ma'mur-e gomrok | مامور گمرک |
| bodyguard | mohāfez-e šaxsi | محافظ شخصی |
| prison guard | negahbān zendān | نگهبان زندان |
| inspector | bāzres | بازرس |

| sportsman | varzeškār | ورزشکار |
| trainer, coach | morabbi | مربی |
| butcher | qassāb | قصاب |
| cobbler (shoe repairer) | kaffāš | کفاش |
| merchant | bāzargān | بازرگان |
| loader (person) | bārbar | باربر |

| fashion designer | tarrāh-e lebas | طراح لباس |
| model (fem.) | model-e zan | مدل زن |

## 93. Occupations. Social status

| schoolboy | dāneš-āmuz | دانش آموز |
| student (college ~) | dānešju | دانشجو |

| philosopher | filsuf | فیلسوف |
| economist | eqtesāddān | اقتصاددان |
| inventor | moxtare' | مخترع |

| unemployed (n) | bikār | بیکار |
| retiree | bāznešaste | بازنشسته |
| spy, secret agent | jāsus | جاسوس |

| prisoner | zendāni | زندانی |
| striker | e'tesāb konande | اعتصاب کننده |
| bureaucrat | ma'mur-e edāri | مأمور اداری |
| traveler (globetrotter) | mosāfer | مسافر |
| gay, homosexual (n) | hamjens-e bāz | همجنس باز |

| | | |
|---|---|---|
| hacker | haker | هکر |
| hippie | hipi | هیپی |
| | | |
| bandit | rāhzan | راهزن |
| hit man, killer | ādamkoš | آدمکش |
| drug addict | mo'tād | معتاد |
| drug dealer | forušande-ye mavādd-e moxadder | فروشندۀ مواد مخدر |
| | | |
| prostitute (fem.) | fāheše | فاحشه |
| pimp | jākeš | جاکش |
| | | |
| sorcerer | jādugar | جادوگر |
| sorceress (evil ~) | jādugar | جادوگر |
| pirate | dozd-e daryāyi | دزد دریایی |
| slave | borde | برده |
| samurai | sāmurāyi | سامورایی |
| savage (primitive) | vahši | وحشی |

# Education

## 94. School

| school | madrese | مدرسه |
| principal (headmaster) | modir-e madrese | مدیر مدرسه |
| | | |
| pupil (boy) | dāneš-āmuz | دانش آموز |
| pupil (girl) | dāneš-āmuz | دانش آموز |
| schoolboy | dāneš-āmuz | دانش آموز |
| schoolgirl | dāneš-āmuz | دانش آموز |
| | | |
| to teach (sb) | āmuxtan | آموختن |
| to learn (language, etc.) | yād gereftan | یاد گرفتن |
| to learn by heart | az hefz kardan | از حفظ کردن |
| | | |
| to learn (~ to count, etc.) | yād gereftan | یاد گرفتن |
| to be in school | tahsil kardan | تحصیل کردن |
| to go to school | madrese raftan | مدرسه رفتن |
| | | |
| alphabet | alefbā | الفبا |
| subject (at school) | mabhas | مبحث |
| | | |
| classroom | kelās | کلاس |
| lesson | dars | درس |
| recess | zang-e tafrih | زنگ تفریح |
| school bell | zang | زنگ |
| school desk | miz-e tahrir | میز تحریر |
| chalkboard | taxte-ye siyāh | تخته سیاه |
| | | |
| grade | nomre | نمره |
| good grade | nomre-ye xub | نمرهٔ خوب |
| bad grade | nomre-ye bad | نمرهٔ بد |
| to give a grade | nomre gozāštan | نمره گذاشتن |
| | | |
| mistake, error | eštebāh | اشتباه |
| to make mistakes | eštebāh kardan | اشتباه کردن |
| to correct (an error) | eslāh kardan | اصلاح کردن |
| cheat sheet | taqallob | تقلب |
| | | |
| homework | taklif manzel | تکلیف منزل |
| exercise (in education) | tamrin | تمرین |
| | | |
| to be present | hozur dāštan | حضور داشتن |
| to be absent | qāyeb budan | غایب بودن |
| to miss school | az madrese qāyeb budan | ازمدرسه غایب بودن |

| to punish (vt) | tanbih kardan | تنبیه کردن |
| punishment | tanbih | تنبیه |
| conduct (behavior) | raftār | رفتار |

| report card | gozāreš-e ruzāne | گزارش روزانه |
| pencil | medād | مداد |
| eraser | pāk kon | پاک کن |
| chalk | gač | گچ |
| pencil case | qalamdān | قلمدان |

| schoolbag | kif madrese | کیف مدرسه |
| pen | xodkār | خودکار |
| school notebook | daftar | دفتر |
| textbook | ketāb-e darsi | کتاب درسی |
| compasses | pargār | پرگار |

| to make technical drawings | rasm kardan | رسم کردن |
| technical drawing | rasm-e fani | رسم فنی |

| poem | še'r | شعر |
| by heart (adv) | az hefz | از حفظ |
| to learn by heart | az hefz kardan | از حفظ کردن |

| school vacation | ta'tilāt | تعطیلات |
| to be on vacation | dar ta'tilāt budan | در تعطیلات بودن |
| to spend one's vacation | ta'tilāt rā gozarāndan | تعطیلات را گذراندن |

| test (written math ~) | emtehān | امتحان |
| essay (composition) | enšā' | انشاء |
| dictation | dikte | دیکته |
| exam (examination) | emtehān | امتحان |
| to take an exam | emtehān dādan | امتحان دادن |
| experiment (e.g., chemistry ~) | āzmāyeš | آزمایش |

## 95. College. University

| academy | farhangestān | فرهنگستان |
| university | dānešgāh | دانشگاه |
| faculty (e.g., ~ of Medicine) | dāneškade | دانشکده |

| student (masc.) | dānešju | دانشجو |
| student (fem.) | dānešju | دانشجو |
| lecturer (teacher) | ostād | استاد |

| lecture hall, room | kelās | کلاس |
| graduate | fāreqottahsil | فارغ التحصیل |
| diploma | diplom | دیپلم |

| | | |
|---|---|---|
| dissertation | pāyān nāme | پایان نامه |
| study (report) | tahqiqe elmi | تحقیق علمی |
| laboratory | āzmāyešgāh | آزمایشگاه |
| | | |
| lecture | soxanrāni | سخنرانی |
| coursemate | ha mdowre i | هم دوره ای |
| scholarship | burse tahsili | بورس تحصیلی |
| academic degree | daraje-ye elmi | درجهٔ علمی |

## 96. Sciences. Disciplines

| | | |
|---|---|---|
| mathematics | riyāziyāt | ریاضیات |
| algebra | jabr | جبر |
| geometry | hendese | هندسه |
| | | |
| astronomy | setāre-šenāsi | ستاره شناسی |
| biology | zist-šenāsi | زیست شناسی |
| geography | joqrāfiyā | جغرافیا |
| geology | zamin-šenāsi | زمین شناسی |
| history | tārix | تاریخ |
| | | |
| medicine | pezeški | پزشکی |
| pedagogy | olume tarbiyati | علوم تربیتی |
| law | hoquq | حقوق |
| | | |
| physics | fizik | فیزیک |
| chemistry | šimi | شیمی |
| philosophy | falsafe | فلسفه |
| psychology | ravānšenāsi | روانشناسی |

## 97. Writing system. Orthography

| | | |
|---|---|---|
| grammar | gerāmer | گرامر |
| vocabulary | vājegān | واژگان |
| phonetics | sadā-šenāsi | صداشناسی |
| | | |
| noun | esm | اسم |
| adjective | sefat | صفت |
| verb | fe'l | فعل |
| adverb | qeyd | قید |
| | | |
| pronoun | zamir | ضمیر |
| interjection | harf-e nedā | حرف ندا |
| preposition | harf-e ezāfe | حرف اضافه |
| | | |
| root | riše-ye kalame | ریشه کلمه |
| ending | pasvand | پسوند |
| prefix | pišvand | پیشوند |

| | | |
|---|---|---|
| syllable | hejā | هجا |
| suffix | pasvand | پسوند |
| stress mark | fešar-e hejā | فشار هجا |
| apostrophe | āpostrof | آپوستروف |
| period, dot | noqte | نقطه |
| comma | virgul | ویرگول |
| semicolon | noqte virgul | نقطه ویرگول |
| colon | donoqte | دونقطه |
| ellipsis | čand noqte | چند نقطه |
| question mark | alāmat-e soāl | علامت سؤال |
| exclamation point | alāmat-e taajjob | علامت تعجب |
| quotation marks | giyume | گیومه |
| in quotation marks | dar giyume | در گیومه |
| parenthesis | parāntez | پرانتز |
| in parenthesis | dar parāntez | در پرانتز |
| hyphen | xatt-e vāsel | خط واصل |
| dash | xatt-e tire | خط تیره |
| space (between words) | fāsele | فاصله |
| letter | harf | حرف |
| capital letter | harf-e bozorg | حرف بزرگ |
| vowel (n) | sedādār | صدادار |
| consonant (n) | sāmet | صامت |
| sentence | jomle | جمله |
| subject | nahād | نهاد |
| predicate | gozāre | گزاره |
| line | satr | سطر |
| on a new line | sar-e satr | سر سطر |
| paragraph | band | بند |
| word | kalame | کلمه |
| group of words | ebārat | عبارت |
| expression | bayān | بیان |
| synonym | moterādef | مترادف |
| antonym | motezād | متضاد |
| rule | qā'ede | قاعده |
| exception | estesnā | استثنا |
| correct (adj) | sahih | صحیح |
| conjugation | sarf | صرف |
| declension | sarf-e kalemāt | صرف کلمات |
| nominal case | hālat | حالت |
| question | soāl | سؤال |

to underline (vt)          xatt kešidan          خط کشیدن
dotted line                noqte čin             نقطه چین

## 98. Foreign languages

| | | |
|---|---|---|
| language | zabān | زبان |
| foreign (adj) | xāreji | خارجی |
| foreign language | zabān-e xāreji | زبان خارجی |
| to study (vt) | dars xāndan | درس خواندن |
| to learn (language, etc.) | yād gereftan | یاد گرفتن |
| to read (vi, vt) | xāndan | خواندن |
| to speak (vi, vt) | harf zadan | حرف زدن |
| to understand (vt) | fahmidan | فهمیدن |
| to write (vt) | neveštan | نوشتن |
| fast (adv) | sari' | سریع |
| slowly (adv) | āheste | آهسته |
| fluently (adv) | ravān | روان |
| rules | qavā'ed | قواعد |
| grammar | gerāmer | گرامر |
| vocabulary | vājegān | واژگان |
| phonetics | āvā-šenāsi | آواشناسی |
| textbook | ketāb-e darsi | کتاب درسی |
| dictionary | farhang-e loqat | فرهنگ لغت |
| teach-yourself book | xod-āmuz | خودآموز |
| phrasebook | ketāb-e mokāleme | کتاب مکالمه |
| cassette, tape | kāst | کاست |
| videotape | kāst-e video | کاست ویدئو |
| CD, compact disc | si-di | سیدی |
| DVD | dey vey dey | دی وی دی |
| alphabet | alefbā | الفبا |
| to spell (vt) | heji kardan | هجی کردن |
| pronunciation | talaffoz | تلفظ |
| accent | lahje | لهجه |
| with an accent | bā lahje | با لهجه |
| without an accent | bi lahje | بی لهجه |
| word | kalame | کلمه |
| meaning | ma'ni | معنی |
| course (e.g., a French ~) | dowre | دوره |
| to sign up | nām-nevisi kardan | نام نویسی کردن |
| teacher | ostād | استاد |
| translation (process) | tarjome | ترجمه |

| translation (text, etc.) | tarjome | ترجمه |
| translator | motarjem | مترجم |
| interpreter | motarjem-e šafāhi | مترجم شفاهی |
| polyglot | čand zabāni | چند زبانی |
| memory | hāfeze | حافظه |

# Rest. Entertainment. Travel

## 99. Trip. Travel

| | | |
|---|---|---|
| tourism, travel | gardešgari | گردشگری |
| tourist | turist | توریست |
| trip, voyage | mosāferat | مسافرت |
| | | |
| adventure | mājarā | ماجرا |
| trip, journey | safar | سفر |
| | | |
| vacation | moraxxasi | مرخصی |
| to be on vacation | dar moraxassi budan | در مرخصی بودن |
| rest | esterāhat | استراحت |
| | | |
| train | qatār | قطار |
| by train | bā qatār | با قطار |
| airplane | havāpeymā | هواپیما |
| by airplane | bā havāpeymā | با هواپیما |
| | | |
| by car | bā otomobil | با اتومبیل |
| by ship | dar kešti | با کشتی |
| | | |
| luggage | bār | بار |
| suitcase | čamedān | چمدان |
| luggage cart | čarx-e hamle bar | چرخ حمل بار |
| | | |
| passport | gozarnāme | گذرنامه |
| visa | ravādid | روادید |
| | | |
| ticket | belit | بلیط |
| air ticket | belit-e havāpeymā | بلیط هواپیما |
| | | |
| guidebook | ketāb-e rāhnamā | کتاب راهنما |
| map (tourist ~) | naqše | نقشه |
| | | |
| area (rural ~) | mahal | محل |
| place, site | jā | جا |
| | | |
| exotica (n) | qarāyeb | غرایب |
| exotic (adj) | qarib | غریب |
| amazing (adj) | heyrat angiz | حیرت انگیز |
| | | |
| group | goruh | گروه |
| excursion, sightseeing tour | gardeš | گردش |
| guide (person) | rāhnamā-ye tur | راهنمای تور |

## 100. Hotel

| | | |
|---|---|---|
| hotel | hotel | هتل |
| motel | motel | متل |
| | | |
| three-star (~ hotel) | se setāre | سه ستاره |
| five-star | panj setāre | پنج ستاره |
| to stay (in a hotel, etc.) | māndan | ماندن |
| | | |
| room | otāq | اتاق |
| single room | otāq-e yeknafare | اتاق یک نفره |
| double room | otāq-e do nafare | اتاق دو نفره |
| to book a room | otāq rezerv kardan | اتاق رزرو کردن |
| | | |
| half board | nim pānsiyon | نیم پانسیون |
| full board | pānsiyon | پانسیون |
| | | |
| with bath | bā vān | با وان |
| with shower | bā duš | با دوش |
| satellite television | televiziyon-e māhvārei | تلویزیون ماهواره ای |
| air-conditioner | tahviye-ye matbu' | تهویه مطبوع |
| towel | howle | حوله |
| key | kelid | کلید |
| | | |
| administrator | edāre-ye konande | اداره کننده |
| chambermaid | mostaxdem | مستخدم |
| porter, bellboy | bārbar | باربر |
| doorman | darbān | دربان |
| | | |
| restaurant | resturān | رستوران |
| pub, bar | bār | بار |
| breakfast | sobhāne | صبحانه |
| dinner | šām | شام |
| buffet | bufe | بوفه |
| | | |
| lobby | lābi | لابی |
| elevator | āsānsor | آسانسور |
| | | |
| DO NOT DISTURB | mozāhem našavid | مزاحم نشوید |
| NO SMOKING | sigār kešidan mamnu' | سیگار کشیدن ممنوع |

# TECHNICAL EQUIPMENT. TRANSPORTATION

## Technical equipment

### 101. Computer

| | | |
|---|---|---|
| computer | kāmpiyuter | کامپیوتر |
| notebook, laptop | lap tāp | لپ تاپ |
| to turn on | rowšan kardan | روشن کردن |
| to turn off | xāmuš kardan | خاموش کردن |
| keyboard | sahfe kelid | صفحه کلید |
| key | kelid | کلید |
| mouse | māows | ماوس |
| mouse pad | māows pad | ماوس پد |
| button | dokme | دکمه |
| cursor | makān namā | مکان نما |
| monitor | monitor | مونیتور |
| screen | safhe | صفحه |
| hard disk | hārd disk | هارد دیسک |
| hard disk capacity | hajm-e hard | حجم هارد |
| memory | hāfeze | حافظه |
| random access memory | hāfeze-ye ram | حافظه رم |
| file | parvande | پرونده |
| folder | puše | پوشه |
| to open (vt) | bāz kardan | باز کردن |
| to close (vt) | bastan | بستن |
| to save (vt) | zaxire kardan | ذخیره کردن |
| to delete (vt) | hazf kardan | حذف کردن |
| to copy (vt) | kopi kardan | کپی کردن |
| to sort (vt) | tabaqe bandi kardan | طبقه بندی کردن |
| to transfer (copy) | kopi kardan | کپی کردن |
| program | barnāme | برنامه |
| software | narm afzār | نرم افزار |
| programmer | barnāme-ye nevis | برنامه نویس |
| to program (vt) | barnāme-nevisi kardan | برنامه نویسی کردن |
| hacker | haker | هکر |
| password | kalame-ye obur | کلمه عبور |

| virus | virus | ویروس |
|---|---|---|
| to find, to detect | peydā kardan | پیدا کردن |

| byte | bāyt | بایت |
|---|---|---|
| megabyte | megābāyt | مگابایت |

| data | dāde-hā | داده ها |
|---|---|---|
| database | pāygāh dāde-hā | پایگاه داده ها |

| cable (USB, etc.) | kābl | کابل |
|---|---|---|
| to disconnect (vt) | jodā kardan | جدا کردن |
| to connect (sth to sth) | vasl kardan | وصل کردن |

## 102. Internet. E-mail

| Internet | internet | اینترنت |
|---|---|---|
| browser | morurgar | مرورگر |
| search engine | motor-e jostoju | موتور جستجو |
| provider | erāe-ye dehande | ارائه دهنده |

| webmaster | tarrāh-e vebsāyt | طراح وب سایت |
|---|---|---|
| website | veb-sāyt | وب سایت |
| webpage | safhe-ye veb | صفحه وب |

| address (e-mail ~) | nešāni | نشانی |
|---|---|---|
| address book | daftarče-ye nešāni | دفترچه نشانی |

| mailbox | sanduq-e post | صندوق پست |
|---|---|---|
| mail | post | پست |
| full (adj) | por | پر |

| message | payām | پیام |
|---|---|---|
| incoming messages | payāmhā-ye vorudi | پیامهای ورودی |
| outgoing messages | payāmhā-ye xoruji | پیامهای خروجی |

| sender | ferestande | فرستنده |
|---|---|---|
| to send (vt) | ferestādan | فرستادن |
| sending (of mail) | ersāl | ارسال |

| receiver | girande | گیرنده |
|---|---|---|
| to receive (vt) | gereftan | گرفتن |

| correspondence | mokātebe | مکاتبه |
|---|---|---|
| to correspond (vi) | mokātebe kardan | مکاتبه کردن |

| file | parvande | پرونده |
|---|---|---|
| to download (vt) | dānlod kardan | دانلود کردن |
| to create (vt) | ijād kardan | ایجاد کردن |
| to delete (vt) | hazf kardan | حذف کردن |
| deleted (adj) | hazf šode | حذف شده |

| connection (ADSL, etc.) | ertebāt | ارتباط |
| speed | sor'at | سرعت |
| modem | modem | مودم |
| access | dastyābi | دستیابی |
| port (e.g., input ~) | dargāh | درگاه |

| connection (make a ~) | ertebāt | ارتباط |
| to connect to ... (vi) | vasl šodan | وصل شدن |

| to select (vt) | entexāb kardan | انتخاب کردن |
| to search (for ...) | jostoju kardan | جستجو کردن |

## 103. Electricity

| electricity | barq | برق |
| electric, electrical (adj) | barqi | برقی |
| electric power plant | nirugāh | نیروگاه |
| energy | enerži | انرژی |
| electric power | niru-ye barq | نیروی برق |

| light bulb | lāmp | لامپ |
| flashlight | čerāq-e dasti | چراغ دستی |
| street light | čerāq-e barq | چراغ برق |

| light | nur | نور |
| to turn on | rowšan kardan | روشن کردن |
| to turn off | xāmuš kardan | خاموش کردن |
| to turn off the light | čerāq rā xāmuš kardan | چراغ را خاموش کردن |

| to burn out (vi) | suxtan | سوختن |
| short circuit | ettesāli | اتصالی |
| broken wire | sim qat' šode | سیم قطع شده |
| contact (electrical ~) | tamās | تماس |

| light switch | kelid | کلید |
| wall socket | periz | پریز |
| plug | došāxe | دوشاخه |
| extension cord | sim-e sayār | سیم سیار |

| fuse | fiyuz | فیوز |
| cable, wire | sim | سیم |
| wiring | sim keši | سیم کشی |

| ampere | āmper | آمپر |
| amperage | šeddat-e jaryān | شدت جریان |
| volt | volt | ولت |
| voltage | voltāž | ولتاژ |

| electrical device | vasile-ye barqi | وسیله برقی |
| indicator | šāxes | شاخص |

| electrician | barq-e kār | برق کار |
| to solder (vt) | lahim kardan | لحیم کردن |
| soldering iron | hoviye | هویه |
| electric current | jaryān-e barq | جریان برق |

## 104. Tools

| tool, instrument | abzār | ابزار |
| tools | abzār | ابزار |
| equipment (factory ~) | tajhizāt | تجهیزات |

| hammer | čakoš | چکش |
| screwdriver | pič gušti | پیچ گوشتی |
| ax | tabar | تبر |

| saw | arre | اره |
| to saw (vt) | arre kardan | اره کردن |
| plane (tool) | rande | رنده |
| to plane (vt) | rande kardan | رنده کردن |
| soldering iron | hoviye | هویه |
| to solder (vt) | lahim kardan | لحیم کردن |

| file (tool) | sowhān | سوهان |
| carpenter pincers | gāzanbor | گازانبر |
| lineman's pliers | anbordast | انبردست |
| chisel | eskene | اسکنه |

| drill bit | sar-matte | سرمته |
| electric drill | matte barqi | مته برقی |
| to drill (vi, vt) | surāx kardan | سوراخ کردن |

| knife | kārd | کارد |
| pocket knife | čāqu-ye jibi | چاقوی جیبی |
| blade | tiqe | تیغه |

| sharp (blade, etc.) | tiz | تیز |
| dull, blunt (adj) | konad | کند |
| to get blunt (dull) | konad šodan | کند شدن |
| to sharpen (vt) | tiz kardan | تیز کردن |

| bolt | pič | پیچ |
| nut | mohre | مهره |
| thread (of a screw) | šiyār | شیار |
| wood screw | pič | پیچ |

| nail | mix | میخ |
| nailhead | sar-e mix | سر میخ |

| ruler (for measuring) | xat keš | خط کش |
| tape measure | metr | متر |

| | | |
|---|---|---|
| spirit level | tarāz | تراز |
| magnifying glass | zarre bin | ذره بین |
| | | |
| measuring instrument | abzār-e andāzegir-i | ابزاراندازه گیری |
| to measure (vt) | andāze gereftan | اندازه گرفتن |
| scale | safhe-ye modarraj | صفحهٔ مدرج |
| (of thermometer, etc.) | | |
| readings | dastgāh-e xaneš | دستگاه خوانش |
| | | |
| compressor | komperesor | کمپرسور |
| microscope | mikroskop | میکروسکوپ |
| | | |
| pump (e.g., water ~) | pomp | پمپ |
| robot | robāt | روبات |
| laser | leyzer | لیزر |
| | | |
| wrench | āčār | آچار |
| adhesive tape | navār-e časb | نوار چسب |
| glue | časb | چسب |
| | | |
| sandpaper | kāqaz-e sonbāde | کاغذ سنباده |
| spring | fanar | فنر |
| magnet | āhan-e robā | آهن ربا |
| gloves | dastkeš | دستکش |
| | | |
| rope | tanāb | طناب |
| cord | band | بند |
| wire (e.g., telephone ~) | sim | سیم |
| cable | kābl | کابل |
| | | |
| sledgehammer | potk | پتک |
| prybar | deylam | دیلم |
| ladder | nardebān | نردبان |
| stepladder | nardebān-e sabok | نردبان سبک |
| | | |
| to screw (tighten) | pič kardan | پیچ کردن |
| to unscrew (lid, filter, etc.) | bāz kardan | باز کردن |
| to tighten | fešordan | فشردن |
| (e.g., with a clamp) | | |
| to glue, to stick | časbāndan | چسباندن |
| to cut (vt) | boridan | بریدن |
| | | |
| malfunction (fault) | xarābi | خرابی |
| repair (mending) | ta'mir | تعمیر |
| to repair, to fix (vt) | ta'mir kardan | تعمیر کردن |
| to adjust (machine, etc.) | tanzim kardan | تنظیم کردن |
| | | |
| to check (to examine) | barresi kardan | بررسی کردن |
| checking | barresi | بررسی |
| readings | dastgāh-e xaneš | دستگاه خوانش |
| reliable, solid (machine) | motmaen | مطمئن |
| complex (adj) | pičide | پیچیده |

| to rust (get rusted) | zang zadan | زنگ زدن |
| rusty, rusted (adj) | zang zade | زنگ زده |
| rust | zang | زنگ |

# Transportation

## 105. Airplane

|  |  |  |
|---|---|---|
| airplane | havāpeymā | هواپیما |
| air ticket | belit-e havāpeymā | بلیط هواپیما |
| airline | šerkat-e havāpeymāyi | شرکت هواپیمایی |
| airport | forudgāh | فرودگاه |
| supersonic (adj) | māvarā sowt | ماوراء صوت |
| captain | kāpitān | کاپیتان |
| crew | xadame | خدمه |
| pilot | xalabān | خلبان |
| flight attendant (fem.) | mehmāndār-e havāpeymā | مهماندار هواپیما |
| navigator | nāvbar | ناویر |
| wings | bāl-hā | بال ها |
| tail | dam | دم |
| cockpit | kābin | کابین |
| engine | motor | موتور |
| undercarriage (landing gear) | šāssi | شاسی |
| turbine | turbin | توربین |
| propeller | parvāne | پروانه |
| black box | ja'be-ye siyāh | جعبه سیاه |
| yoke (control column) | farmān | فرمان |
| fuel | suxt | سوخت |
| safety card | dasturol'amal | دستورالعمل |
| oxygen mask | māsk-e oksižen | ماسک اکسیژن |
| uniform | oniform | اونیفورم |
| life vest | jeliqe-ye nejāt | جلیقة نجات |
| parachute | čatr-e nejāt | چترنجات |
| takeoff | parvāz | پرواز |
| to take off (vi) | parvāz kardan | پرواز کردن |
| runway | bānd-e forudgāh | باند فرودگاه |
| visibility | meydān did | میدان دید |
| flight (act of flying) | parvāz | پرواز |
| altitude | ertefā' | ارتفاع |
| air pocket | čāle-ye havāyi | چاله هوایی |
| seat | jā | جا |
| headphones | guši | گوشی |

| folding tray (tray table) | sini-ye tāšow | سینی تاشو |
| airplane window | panjere | پنجره |
| aisle | rāhrow | راهرو |

## 106. Train

| train | qatār | قطار |
| commuter train | qatār-e barqi | قطار برقی |
| express train | qatār-e sari'osseyr | قطار سریع السیر |
| diesel locomotive | lokomotiv-e dizel | لوکوموتیو دیزل |
| steam locomotive | lokomotiv-e boxar | لوکوموتیو بخار |

| passenger car | vāgon | واگن |
| dining car | vāgon-e resturān | واگن رستوران |

| rails | reyl-hā | ریل ها |
| railroad | rāh āhan | راه آهن |
| railway tie | reyl-e band | ریل بند |

| platform (railway ~) | sakku-ye rāh-āhan | سکوی راه آهن |
| track (~ 1, 2, etc.) | masir | مسیر |
| semaphore | nešanar | نشانبر |
| station | istgāh | ایستگاه |

| engineer (train driver) | rānande | راننده |
| porter (of luggage) | bārbar | باربر |
| car attendant | rāhnamā-ye qatār | راهنمای قطار |
| passenger | mosāfer | مسافر |
| conductor | kontorol či | کنترل چی |
| (ticket inspector) | | |

| corridor (in train) | rāhrow | راهرو |
| emergency brake | tormoz-e ezterāri | ترمز اضطراری |

| compartment | kupe | کوپه |
| berth | taxt-e kupe | تخت کوپه |
| upper berth | taxt-e bālā | تخت بالا |
| lower berth | taxt-e pāyin | تخت پایین |
| bed linen, bedding | raxt-e xāb | رخت خواب |

| ticket | belit | بلیط |
| schedule | barnāme | برنامه |
| information display | barnāme-ye zamāni | برنامه زمانی |

| to leave, to depart | tark kardan | ترک کردن |
| departure (of train) | harekat | حرکت |
| to arrive (ab. train) | residan | رسیدن |
| arrival | vorud | ورود |
| to arrive by train | bā qatār āmadan | با قطار آمدن |
| to get on the train | savār-e qatār šodan | سوار قطار شدن |

| to get off the train | az qatār piyāde šodan | از قطار پیاده شدن |
| train wreck | sānehe | سانحه |
| to derail (vi) | az xat xārej šodan | از خط خارج شدن |

| steam locomotive | lokomotiv-e boxar | لوکوموتیو بخار |
| stoker, fireman | ātaškār | آتشکار |
| firebox | ātašdān | آتشدان |
| coal | zoqāl sang | زغال سنگ |

## 107. Ship

| ship | kešti | کشتی |
| vessel | kešti | کشتی |

| steamship | kešti-ye boxāri | کشتی بخاری |
| riverboat | qāyeq-e rudxāne | قایق رودخانه |
| cruise ship | kešti-ye tafrihi | کشتی تفریحی |
| cruiser | razm nāv | رزم ناو |

| yacht | qāyeq-e tafrihi | قایق تفریحی |
| tugboat | yadak keš | یدک کش |
| barge | kešti-ye bārkeše yadaki | کشتی بارکش یدکی |
| ferry | kešti-ye farābar | کشتی فرابر |

| sailing ship | kešti-ye bādbāni | کشتی بادبانی |
| brigantine | košti dozdān daryā-yi | کشتی دزدان دریایی |

| ice breaker | kešti-ye yaxšekan | کشتی یخ شکن |
| submarine | zirdaryāyi | زیردریایی |

| boat (flat-bottomed ~) | qāyeq | قایق |
| dinghy | qāyeq-e tafrihi | قایق تفریحی |
| lifeboat | qāyeq-e nejāt | قایق نجات |
| motorboat | qāyeq-e motori | قایق موتوری |

| captain | kāpitān | کاپیتان |
| seaman | malavān | ملوان |
| sailor | malavān | ملوان |
| crew | xadame | خدمه |

| boatswain | sar malavān | سر ملوان |
| ship's boy | šāgerd-e malavān | شاگرد ملوان |
| cook | āšpaz-e kešti | آشپز کشتی |
| ship's doctor | pezešk-e kešti | پزشک کشتی |

| deck | arše-ye kešti | عرشهٔ کشتی |
| mast | dakal | دکل |
| sail | bādbān | بادبان |
| hold | anbār | انبار |
| bow (prow) | sine-ye kešti | سینه کشتی |

| | | |
|---|---|---|
| stern | aqab kešti | عقب کشتی |
| oar | pāru | پارو |
| screw propeller | parvāne | پروانه |
| cabin | otāq-e kešti | اتاق کشتی |
| wardroom | otāq-e afsarān | اتاق افسران |
| engine room | motor xāne | موتور خانه |
| bridge | pol-e farmāndehi | پل فرماندهی |
| radio room | kābin-e bisim | کابین بی سیم |
| wave (radio) | mowj | موج |
| logbook | roxdād nāme | رخداد نامه |
| spyglass | teleskop | تلسکوپ |
| bell | nāqus | ناقوس |
| flag | parčam | پرچم |
| hawser (mooring ~) | tanāb | طناب |
| knot (bowline, etc.) | gereh | گره |
| deckrails | narde | نرده |
| gangway | pol | پل |
| anchor | langar | لنگر |
| to weigh anchor | langar kešidan | لنگر کشیدن |
| to drop anchor | langar andāxtan | لنگر انداختن |
| anchor chain | zanjir-e langar | زنجیر لنگر |
| port (harbor) | bandar | بندر |
| quay, wharf | eskele | اسکله |
| to berth (moor) | pahlu gereftan | پهلو گرفتن |
| to cast off | tark kardan | ترک کردن |
| trip, voyage | mosāferat | مسافرت |
| cruise (sea trip) | safar-e daryāyi | سفر دریایی |
| course (route) | masir | مسیر |
| route (itinerary) | masir | مسیر |
| fairway (safe water channel) | kešti-ye ru | کشتی رو |
| shallows | mahall-e kam omq | محل کم عمق |
| to run aground | be gel nešastan | به گل نشستن |
| storm | tufān | طوفان |
| signal | alāmat | علامت |
| to sink (vi) | qarq šodan | غرق شدن |
| Man overboard! | kas-i dar hāl-e qarq šodan-ast! | کسی در حال غرق شدن است! |
| SOS (distress signal) | sos | SOS |
| ring buoy | kamarband-e nejāt | کمربند نجات |

## 108. Airport

|  |  |  |
|---|---|---|
| airport | forudgāh | فرودگاه |
| airplane | havāpeymā | هواپیما |
| airline | šerkat-e havāpeymāyi | شرکت هواپیمایی |
| air traffic controller | ma'mur-e kontorol-e terāfik-e havāyi | مأمور کنترل ترافیک هوایی |
| departure | azimat | عزیمت |
| arrival | vorud | ورود |
| to arrive (by plane) | residan | رسیدن |
| departure time | zamān-e parvāz | زمان پرواز |
| arrival time | zamān-e vorud | زمان ورود |
| to be delayed | ta'xir kardan | تأخیر کردن |
| flight delay | ta'xir-e parvāz | تأخیر پرواز |
| information board | tāblo-ye ettelā'āt | تابلوی اطلاعات |
| information | ettelā'āt | اطلاعات |
| to announce (vt) | e'lām kardan | اعلام کردن |
| flight (e.g., next ~) | parvāz | پرواز |
| customs | gomrok | گمرک |
| customs officer | ma'mur-e gomrok | مأمور گمرک |
| customs declaration | ežhār-nāme | اظهارنامه |
| to fill out (vt) | por kardan | پر کردن |
| to fill out the declaration | ežhār-nāme rā por kardan | اظهارنامه را پر کردن |
| passport control | kontorol-e gozarnāme | کنترل گذرنامه |
| luggage | bār | بار |
| hand luggage | bār-e dasti | بار دستی |
| luggage cart | čarx-e hamle bar | چرخ حمل بار |
| landing | forud | فرود |
| landing strip | bānd-e forudgāh | باند فرودگاه |
| to land (vi) | nešastan | نشستن |
| airstairs | pellekān | پلکان |
| check-in | ček in | چک این |
| check-in counter | bāje-ye kontorol | باجه کنترل |
| to check-in (vi) | čekin kardan | چکاین کردن |
| boarding pass | kārt-e parvāz | کارت پرواز |
| departure gate | gi-yat xoruj | گیت خروج |
| transit | terānzit | ترانزیت |
| to wait (vt) | montazer budan | منتظر بودن |
| departure lounge | tālār-e entezār | تالار انتظار |
| to see off | badraqe kardan | بدرقه کردن |
| to say goodbye | xodāhāfezi kardan | خداحافظی کردن |

# Life events

## 109. Holidays. Event

| | | |
|---|---|---|
| celebration, holiday | jašn | جشن |
| national day | eyd-e melli | عید ملی |
| public holiday | ruz-e jašn | روز جشن |
| to commemorate (vt) | jašn gereftan | جشن گرفتن |
| | | |
| event (happening) | vāqe'e | واقعه |
| event (organized activity) | ruydād | رویداد |
| banquet (party) | ziyāfat | ضیافت |
| reception (formal party) | ziyāfat | ضیافت |
| feast | jašn | جشن |
| | | |
| anniversary | sālgard | سالگرد |
| jubilee | sālgard | سالگرد |
| to celebrate (vt) | jašn gereftan | جشن گرفتن |
| | | |
| New Year | sāl-e now | سال نو |
| Happy New Year! | sāl-e now mobārak | سال نو مبارک |
| Santa Claus | bābā noel | بابا نوئل |
| | | |
| Christmas | kerismas | کریسمس |
| Merry Christmas! | kerismas mobārak! | کریسمس مبارک! |
| Christmas tree | kāj kerismas | کاج کریسمس |
| fireworks (fireworks show) | ātaš-e bāzi | آتش بازی |
| | | |
| wedding | arusi | عروسی |
| groom | dāmād | داماد |
| bride | arus | عروس |
| | | |
| to invite (vt) | da'vat kardan | دعوت کردن |
| invitation card | da'vatnāme | دعوتنامه |
| | | |
| guest | mehmān | مهمان |
| to visit | be mehmāni raftan | به مهمانی رفتن |
| (~ your parents, etc.) | | |
| to meet the guests | az mehmānān esteqbāl kardan | از مهمانان استقبال کردن |
| | | |
| gift, present | hedye | هدیه |
| to give (sth as present) | hadye dādan | هدیه دادن |
| to receive gifts | hediye gereftan | هدیه گرفتن |
| bouquet (of flowers) | daste-ye gol | دسته گل |
| congratulations | tabrik | تبریک |

| | | |
|---|---|---|
| to congratulate (vt) | tabrik goftan | تبریک گفتن |
| greeting card | kārt-e tabrik | کارت تبریک |
| to send a postcard | kārt-e tabrik ferestādan | کارت تبریک فرستادن |
| to get a postcard | kārt-e tabrik gereftan | کارت تبریک گرفتن |
| | | |
| toast | be salāmati-ye kas-i nušidan | به سلامتی کسی نوشیدن |
| to offer (a drink, etc.) | pazirāyi kardan | پذیرایی کردن |
| champagne | šāmpāyn | شامپاین |
| | | |
| to enjoy oneself | šādi kardan | شادی کردن |
| merriment (gaiety) | šādi | شادی |
| joy (emotion) | maserrat | مسرت |
| | | |
| dance | raqs | رقص |
| to dance (vi, vt) | raqsidan | رقصیدن |
| | | |
| waltz | raqs-e vāls | رقص والس |
| tango | raqs tāngo | رقص تانگو |

## 110. Funerals. Burial

| | | |
|---|---|---|
| cemetery | qabrestān | قبرستان |
| grave, tomb | qabr | قبر |
| cross | salib | صلیب |
| gravestone | sang-e qabr | سنگ قبر |
| fence | hesār | حصار |
| chapel | kelisā-ye kučak | کلیسای کوچک |
| | | |
| death | marg | مرگ |
| to die (vi) | mordan | مردن |
| the deceased | marhum | مرحوم |
| mourning | azā | عزا |
| | | |
| to bury (vt) | dafn kardan | دفن کردن |
| funeral home | xadamat-e kafno dafn | خدمات کفن ودفن |
| funeral | tašyi-'e jenāze | تشییع جنازه |
| | | |
| wreath | tāj-e gol | تاج گل |
| casket, coffin | tābut | تابوت |
| hearse | na'š keš | نعش کش |
| shroud | kafan | کفن |
| | | |
| funeral procession | tašyi-'e jenāze | تشییع جنازه |
| funerary urn | zarf-e xākestar-e morde | ظرف خاکستر مرده |
| crematory | morde suz xāne | مرده سوز خانه |
| | | |
| obituary | āgahi-ye tarhim | آگهی ترحیم |
| to cry (weep) | gerye kardan | گریه کردن |
| to sob (vi) | zār zār gerye kardan | زار زارگریه کردن |

## 111. War. Soldiers

| | | |
|---|---|---|
| platoon | daste | دسته |
| company | goruhān | گروهان |
| regiment | hang | هنگ |
| army | arteš | ارتش |
| division | laškar | لشکر |

| | | |
|---|---|---|
| section, squad | daste | دسته |
| host (army) | laškar | لشکر |

| | | |
|---|---|---|
| soldier | sarbāz | سرباز |
| officer | afsar | افسر |

| | | |
|---|---|---|
| private | sarbāz | سرباز |
| sergeant | goruhbān | گروهبان |
| lieutenant | sotvān | ستوان |
| captain | kāpitān | کاپیتان |
| major | sargord | سرگرد |
| colonel | sarhang | سرهنگ |
| general | ženerāl | ژنرال |

| | | |
|---|---|---|
| sailor | malavān | ملوان |
| captain | kāpitān | کاپیتان |
| boatswain | sar malavān | سر ملوان |

| | | |
|---|---|---|
| artilleryman | tupči | توپچی |
| paratrooper | sarbāz-e čatrbāz | سرباز چترباز |
| pilot | xalabān | خلبان |
| navigator | nāvbar | ناوبر |
| mechanic | mekānik | مکانیک |

| | | |
|---|---|---|
| pioneer (sapper) | mohandes estehkāmāt | مهندس استحکامات |
| parachutist | čatr bāz | چترباز |
| reconnaissance scout | ettelā'āti | اطلاعاتی |
| sniper | tak tir andāz | تک تیر انداز |

| | | |
|---|---|---|
| patrol (group) | gašt | گشت |
| to patrol (vt) | gašt zadan | گشت زدن |
| sentry, guard | negahbān | نگهبان |

| | | |
|---|---|---|
| warrior | jangju | جنگجو |
| patriot | mihan parast | میهن پرست |
| hero | qahremān | قهرمان |
| heroine | qahremān-e zan | قهرمان زن |

| | | |
|---|---|---|
| traitor | xāen | خائن |
| to betray (vt) | xiyānat kardan | خیانت کردن |

| | | |
|---|---|---|
| deserter | farāri | فراری |
| to desert (vi) | farāri budan | فراری بودن |

| mercenary | mozdur | مزدور |
| recruit | sarbāz-e jadid | سرباز جدید |
| volunteer | dāvtalab | داوطلب |

| dead (n) | morde | مرده |
| wounded (n) | zaxmi | زخمی |
| prisoner of war | asir | اسیر |

## 112. War. Military actions. Part 1

| war | jang | جنگ |
| to be at war | jangidan | جنگیدن |
| civil war | jang-e dāxeli | جنگ داخلی |

| treacherously (adv) | xāenāne | خائنانه |
| declaration of war | e'lān-e jang | اعلان جنگ |
| to declare (~ war) | e'lān kardan | اعلان کردن |
| aggression | tajāvoz | تجاوز |
| to attack (invade) | hamle kardan | حمله کردن |

| to invade (vt) | tajāvoz kardan | تجاوز کردن |
| invader | tajāvozgar | تجاوزگر |
| conqueror | fāteh | فاتح |

| defense | defā' | دفاع |
| to defend (a country, etc.) | defā' kardan | دفاع کردن |
| to defend (against ...) | az xod defā' kardan | از خود دفاع کردن |

| enemy | došman | دشمن |
| foe, adversary | moxālef | مخالف |
| enemy (as adj) | došman | دشمن |

| strategy | rāhbord | راهبرد |
| tactics | tāktik | تاکتیک |

| order | farmān | فرمان |
| command (order) | dastur | دستور |
| to order (vt) | farmān dādan | فرمان دادن |
| mission | ma'muriyat | مأموریت |
| secret (adj) | mahramāne | محرمانه |

| battle | jang | جنگ |
| combat | nabard | نبرد |

| attack | hamle | حمله |
| charge (assault) | yureš | یورش |
| to storm (vt) | yureš bordan | یورش بردن |
| siege (to be under ~) | mohāsere | محاصره |
| offensive (n) | hamle | حمله |
| to go on the offensive | hamle kardan | حمله کردن |

| | | |
|---|---|---|
| retreat | aqab nešini | عقب نشینی |
| to retreat (vi) | aqab nešini kardan | عقب نشینی کردن |
| | | |
| encirclement | mohāsere | محاصره |
| to encircle (vt) | mohāsere kardan | محاصره کردن |
| | | |
| bombing (by aircraft) | bombārān-e havāyi | بمباران هوایی |
| to drop a bomb | bomb āndaxtan | بمب انداختن |
| to bomb (vt) | bombārān kardan | بمباران کردن |
| explosion | enfejār | انفجار |
| | | |
| shot | tirandāzi | تیراندازی |
| to fire (~ a shot) | tirandāzi kardan | تیراندازی کردن |
| firing (burst of ~) | tirandāzi | تیراندازی |
| | | |
| to aim (to point a weapon) | nešāne raftan | نشانه رفتن |
| to point (a gun) | šhellik kardan | شلیک کردن |
| to hit (the target) | residan | رسیدن |
| | | |
| to sink (~ a ship) | qarq šodan | غرق شدن |
| hole (in a ship) | surāx | سوراخ |
| to founder, to sink (vi) | qarq šodan | غرق شدن |
| | | |
| front (war ~) | jebhe | جبهه |
| evacuation | taxliye | تخلیه |
| to evacuate (vt) | taxliye kardan | تخلیه کردن |
| | | |
| trench | sangar | سنگر |
| barbwire | sim-e xārdār | سیم خاردار |
| barrier (anti tank ~) | hesār | حصار |
| watchtower | borj | برج |
| | | |
| military hospital | bimārestān-e nezāmi | بیمارستان نظامی |
| to wound (vt) | majruh kardan | مجروح کردن |
| wound | zaxm | زخم |
| wounded (n) | zaxmi | زخمی |
| to be wounded | zaxmi šodan | زخمی شدن |
| serious (wound) | zaxm-e saxt | زخم سخت |

## 113. War. Military actions. Part 2

| | | |
|---|---|---|
| captivity | esārat | اسارت |
| to take captive | be esārat gereftan | به اسارت گرفتن |
| to be held captive | dar esārat budan | در اسارت بودن |
| to be taken captive | be esārat oftādan | به اسارت افتادن |
| | | |
| concentration camp | ordugāh-e kār-e ejbāri | اردوگاه کار اجباری |
| prisoner of war | asir | اسیر |
| to escape (vi) | farār kardan | فرار کردن |
| to betray (vt) | xiyānat kardan | خیانت کردن |

| betrayer | xāen | خائن |
| betrayal | xiyānat | خیانت |

| to execute (by firing squad) | tirbārān kardan | تیرباران کردن |
| execution (by firing squad) | tirbārān | تیرباران |

| equipment (military gear) | uniform | یونیفرم |
| shoulder board | daraje-ye sarduši | درجه سردوشی |
| gas mask | māsk-e zedd-e gāz | ماسک ضد گاز |

| field radio | dastgāh-e bisim | دستگاه بی سیم |
| cipher, code | ramz | رمز |
| secrecy | mahramāne budan | محرمانه بودن |
| password | ramz | رمز |

| land mine | min | مین |
| to mine (road, etc.) | min gozāštan | مین گذاشتن |
| minefield | meydān-e min | میدان مین |

| air-raid warning | āžir-e havāyi | آژیر هوایی |
| alarm (alert signal) | āžir | آژیر |
| signal | alāmat | علامت |
| signal flare | monavvar | منور |

| headquarters | setād | ستاد |
| reconnaissance | šenāsāyi | شناسایی |
| situation | vaz'iyat | وضعیت |
| report | gozāreš | گزارش |
| ambush | kamin | کمین |
| reinforcement (of army) | taqviyat | تقویت |

| target | hadaf giri | هدف گیری |
| proving ground | meydān-e tir | میدان تیر |
| military exercise | mānovr | مانور |

| panic | vahšat | وحشت |
| devastation | xarābi | خرابی |
| destruction, ruins | xarābi-hā | خرابی ها |
| to destroy (vt) | xarāb kardan | خراب کردن |

| to survive (vi, vt) | zende māndan | زنده ماندن |
| to disarm (vt) | xal'-e selāh kardan | خلع سلاح کردن |
| to handle (~ a gun) | be kār bordan | به کار بردن |

| Attention! | xabardār! | خبردار! |
| At ease! | āzād! | آزاد! |

| act of courage | delāvari | دلاوری |
| oath (vow) | sowgand | سوگند |
| to swear (an oath) | sowgand xordan | سوگند خوردن |
| decoration (medal, etc.) | pādāš | پاداش |

| to award (give medal to) | medāl dādan | مدال دادن |
| medal | medāl | مدال |
| order (e.g., ~ of Merit) | nešān | نشان |

| victory | piruzi | پیروزی |
| defeat | šekast | شکست |
| armistice | ātaš bas | آتش بس |

| standard (battle flag) | parčam | پرچم |
| glory (honor, fame) | eftexār | افتخار |
| parade | reže | رژه |
| to march (on parade) | reže raftan | رژه رفتن |

## 114. Weapons

| weapons | selāh | سلاح |
| firearms | aslahe-ye garm | اسلحهٔ گرم |
| cold weapons (knives, etc.) | aslahe-ye sard | اسلحهٔ سرد |

| chemical weapons | taslihāt-e šimiyāyi | تسلیحات شیمیایی |
| nuclear (adj) | haste i | هسته ای |
| nuclear weapons | taslihāt-e hastei | تسلیحات هسته ای |

| bomb | bomb | بمب |
| atomic bomb | bomb-e atomi | بمب اتمی |

| pistol (gun) | kolt | کلت |
| rifle | tofang | تفنگ |
| submachine gun | mosalsal-e xodkār | مسلسل خودکار |
| machine gun | mosalsal | مسلسل |

| muzzle | sar-e lule-ye tofang | سر لولۀ تفنگ |
| barrel | lule-ye tofang | لولۀ تفنگ |
| caliber | kālibr | کالیبر |

| trigger | māše | ماشه |
| sight (aiming device) | nešāne ravi | نشانه روی |
| magazine | xešāb | خشاب |
| butt (shoulder stock) | qondāq | قنداق |

| hand grenade | nārenjak | نارنجک |
| explosive | mādde-ye monfajere | مادۀ منفجره |

| bullet | golule | گلوله |
| cartridge | fešang | فشنگ |
| charge | mohemmāt | مهمات |
| ammunition | mohemmāt | مهمات |
| bomber (aircraft) | bomb-afkan | بمبافکن |
| fighter | jangande | جنگنده |

| helicopter | helikopter | هلیکوپتر |
| anti-aircraft gun | tup-e zedd-e havāyi | توپ ضد هوایی |
| tank | tānk | تانک |
| tank gun | tup | توپ |

| artillery | tupxāne | توپخانه |
| gun (cannon, howitzer) | tofang | تفنگ |
| to lay (a gun) | šhellik kardan | شلیک کردن |

| shell (projectile) | xompāre | خمپاره |
| mortar bomb | xompāre | خمپاره |
| mortar | xompāre andāz | خمپاره انداز |
| splinter (shell fragment) | tarkeš | ترکش |

| submarine | zirdaryāyi | زیردریایی |
| torpedo | eždar | اژدر |
| missile | mušak | موشک |

| to load (gun) | por kardan | پر کردن |
| to shoot (vi) | tirandāzi kardan | تیراندازی کردن |
| to point at (the cannon) | nešāne raftan | نشانه رفتن |
| bayonet | sarneyze | سرنیزه |

| rapier | šamšir | شمشیر |
| saber (e.g., cavalry ~) | šamšir | شمشیر |
| spear (weapon) | neyze | نیزه |
| bow | kamān | کمان |
| arrow | tir | تیر |
| musket | tofang fetile-i | تفنگ فتیله‌ای |
| crossbow | kamān zanburak-i | کمان زنبورکی |

## 115. Ancient people

| primitive (prehistoric) | avvaliye | اولیه |
| prehistoric (adj) | piš az tārix | پیش از تاریخ |
| ancient (~ civilization) | qadimi | قدیمی |

| Stone Age | asr-e hajar | عصر حجر |
| Bronze Age | asr-e mafraq | عصر مفرغ |
| Ice Age | dowre-ye yaxbandān | دورهٔ یخبندان |

| tribe | qabile | قبیله |
| cannibal | ādam xār | آدم خوار |
| hunter | šekārči | شکارچی |
| to hunt (vi, vt) | šekār kardan | شکار کردن |
| mammoth | māmut | ماموت |

| cave | qār | غار |
| fire | ātaš | آتش |
| campfire | ātaš | آتش |

| | | |
|---|---|---|
| cave painting | qār negāre | غار نگاره |
| tool (e.g., stone ax) | abzār-e kār | ابزار کار |
| spear | neyze | نیزه |
| stone ax | tabar-e sangi | تبر سنگی |
| to be at war | jangidan | جنگیدن |
| to domesticate (vt) | rām kardan | رام کردن |
| | | |
| idol | bot | بت |
| to worship (vt) | parastidan | پرستیدن |
| superstition | xorāfe | خرافه |
| rite | marāsem | مراسم |
| | | |
| evolution | takāmol | تکامل |
| development | pišraft | پیشرفت |
| disappearance (extinction) | enqerāz | انقراض |
| to adapt oneself | sāzgār šodan | سازگار شدن |
| | | |
| archeology | bāstān-šenāsi | باستان شناسی |
| archeologist | bāstān-šenās | باستان شناس |
| archeological (adj) | bāstān-šenāsi | باستان شناسی |
| | | |
| excavation site | mahall-e haffārihā | محل حفاری ها |
| excavations | haffāri-hā | حفاری ها |
| find (object) | yāfteh | یافته |
| fragment | qet'e | قطعه |

## 116. Middle Ages

| | | |
|---|---|---|
| people (ethnic group) | mellat | ملت |
| peoples | mellat-hā | ملت ها |
| tribe | qabile | قبیله |
| tribes | qabāyel | قبایل |
| | | |
| barbarians | barbar-hā | بربر ها |
| Gauls | gul-hā | گول ها |
| Goths | gat-hā | گت ها |
| Slavs | eslāv-hā | اسلاو ها |
| Vikings | vāyking-hā | وایکینگ ها |
| | | |
| Romans | rumi-hā | رومی ها |
| Roman (adj) | rumi | رومی |
| | | |
| Byzantines | bizānsi-hā | بیزانسی ها |
| Byzantium | bizāns | بیزانس |
| Byzantine (adj) | bizānsi | بیزانسی |
| | | |
| emperor | emperātur | امپراطور |
| leader, chief (tribal ~) | rahbar | رهبر |
| powerful (~ king) | moqtader | مقتدر |
| king | šāh | شاه |

| | | |
|---|---|---|
| ruler (sovereign) | hākem | حاکم |
| knight | šovālie | شوالیه |
| feudal lord | feodāl | فئودال |
| feudal (adj) | feodāli | فئودالی |
| vassal | ra'yat | رعبت |
| | | |
| duke | duk | دوک |
| earl | kont | کنت |
| baron | bāron | بارون |
| bishop | osqof | اسقف |
| | | |
| armor | zereh | زره |
| shield | separ | سپر |
| sword | šamšir | شمشیر |
| visor | labe-ye kolāh | لبه کلاه |
| chainmail | jowšan | جوشن |
| | | |
| Crusade | jang-e salibi | جنگ صلیبی |
| crusader | jangju-ye salibi | جنگجوی صلیبی |
| | | |
| territory | qalamrow | قلمرو |
| to attack (invade) | hamle kardan | حمله کردن |
| to conquer (vt) | fath kardan | فتح کردن |
| to occupy (invade) | ešqāl kardan | اشغال کردن |
| | | |
| siege (to be under ~) | mohāsere | محاصره |
| besieged (adj) | mahsur | محصور |
| to besiege (vt) | mohāsere kardan | محاصره کردن |
| | | |
| inquisition | taftiš-e aqāyed | تفتیش عقاید |
| inquisitor | mofatteš | مفتش |
| torture | šekanje | شکنجه |
| cruel (adj) | bi rahm | بی رحم |
| heretic | molhed | ملحد |
| heresy | ertedād | ارتداد |
| | | |
| seafaring | daryānavardi | دریانوردی |
| pirate | dozd-e daryāyi | دزد دریایی |
| piracy | dozdi-ye daryāyi | دزدی دریایی |
| boarding (attack) | hamle ruye arše | حمله روی عرشه |
| | | |
| loot, booty | qanimat | غنیمت |
| treasures | ganj | گنج |
| | | |
| discovery | kašf | کشف |
| to discover (new land, etc.) | kašf kardan | کشف کردن |
| expedition | safar | سفر |
| | | |
| musketeer | tofangdār | تفنگدار |
| cardinal | kārdināl | کاردینال |
| heraldry | nešān-šenāsi | نشان شناسی |
| heraldic (adj) | manquš | منقوش |

## 117. Leader. Chief. Authorities

| king | šāh | شاه |
| queen | maleke | ملکه |
| royal (adj) | šāhi | شاهی |
| kingdom | pādšāhi | پادشاهی |

| prince | šāhzāde | شاهزاده |
| princess | pranses | پرنسس |

| president | ra'is jomhur | رئیس جمهور |
| vice-president | mo'āven-e rais-e jomhur | معاون رئیس جمهور |
| senator | senātor | سناتور |

| monarch | pādšāh | پادشاه |
| ruler (sovereign) | hākem | حاکم |
| dictator | diktātor | دیکتاتور |
| tyrant | zālem | ظالم |
| magnate | najib zāde | نجیب زاده |

| director | modir | مدیر |
| chief | ra'is | رئیس |
| manager (director) | modir | مدیر |
| boss | ra'is | رئیس |
| owner | sāheb | صاحب |

| leader | rahbar | رهبر |
| head (~ of delegation) | ra'is | رئیس |
| authorities | maqāmāt | مقامات |
| superiors | roasā | رؤسا |

| governor | farmāndār | فرماندار |
| consul | konsul | کنسول |
| diplomat | diplomāt | دیپلمات |
| mayor | šahrdār | شهردار |
| sheriff | kalāntar | کلانتر |

| emperor | emperātur | امپراطور |
| tsar, czar | tezār | تزار |
| pharaoh | fer'own | فرعون |
| khan | xān | خان |

## 118. Breaking the law. Criminals. Part 1

| bandit | rāhzan | راهزن |
| crime | jenāyat | جنایت |
| criminal (person) | jenāyatkār | جنایتکار |
| thief | dozd | دزد |
| to steal (vi, vt) | dozdidan | دزدیدن |

| | | |
|---|---|---|
| stealing (larceny) | dozdi | دزدی |
| theft | serqat | سرقت |
| to kidnap (vt) | ādam robudan | آدم ربودن |
| kidnapping | ādam robāyi | آدم ربایی |
| kidnapper | ādam robā | آدم ربا |
| ransom | bāj | باج |
| to demand ransom | bāj xāstan | باج خواستن |
| to rob (vt) | serqat kardan | سرقت کردن |
| robbery | serqat | سرقت |
| robber | qāratgar | غارتگر |
| to extort (vt) | axxāzi kardan | اخاذی کردن |
| extortionist | axxāz | اخاذ |
| extortion | axxāzi | اخاذی |
| to murder, to kill | koštan | کشتن |
| murder | qatl | قتل |
| murderer | qātel | قاتل |
| gunshot | tirandāzi | تیراندازی |
| to fire (~ a shot) | tirandāzi kardan | تیراندازی کردن |
| to shoot to death | bā tir zadan | با تیر زدن |
| to shoot (vi) | tirandāzi kardan | تیراندازی کردن |
| shooting | tirandāzi | تیراندازی |
| incident (fight, etc.) | vāqeʻe | واقعه |
| fight, brawl | zad-o xord | زد و خورد |
| Help! | komak! | کمک! |
| victim | qorbāni | قربانی |
| to damage (vt) | xesārat resāndan | خسارت رساندن |
| damage | xesārat | خسارت |
| dead body, corpse | jasad | جسد |
| grave (~ crime) | vaxim | وخیم |
| to attack (vt) | hamle kardan | حمله کردن |
| to beat (to hit) | zadan | زدن |
| to beat up | kotak zadan | کتک زدن |
| to take (rob of sth) | bezur gereftan | به زور گرفتن |
| to stab to death | čāqu zadan | چاقو زدن |
| to maim (vt) | maʻyub kardan | معیوب کردن |
| to wound (vt) | majruh kardan | مجروح کردن |
| blackmail | šāntāž | شانتاژ |
| to blackmail (vt) | axxāzi kardan | اخاذی کردن |
| blackmailer | axxāz | اخاذ |
| protection racket | axxāzi | اخاذی |
| racketeer | axxāz | اخاذ |

| gangster | gāngester | گانگستر |
| mafia, Mob | māfiyā | مافیا |

| pickpocket | jib bor | جیب بر |
| burglar | sāreq | سارق |
| smuggling | qāčāq | قاچاق |
| smuggler | qāčāqči | قاچاقچی |

| forgery | qollābi | قلابی |
| to forge (counterfeit) | ja'l kardan | جعل کردن |
| fake (forged) | ja'li | جعلی |

## 119. Breaking the law. Criminals. Part 2

| rape | tajāvoz be nāmus | تجاوز به ناموس |
| to rape (vt) | tajāvoz kardan | تجاوز کردن |
| rapist | zenā konande | زنا کننده |
| maniac | majnun | مجنون |

| prostitute (fem.) | fāheše | فاحشه |
| prostitution | fāhešegi | فاحشگی |
| pimp | jākeš | جاکش |

| drug addict | mo'tād | معتاد |
| drug dealer | forušande-ye mavādd-e moxadder | فروشندهٔ مواد مخدر |

| to blow up (bomb) | monfajer kardan | منفجر کردن |
| explosion | enfejār | انفجار |
| to set fire | ātaš zadan | آتش زدن |
| arsonist | ātaš afruz | آتش افروز |

| terrorism | terorism | تروریسم |
| terrorist | terorist | تروریست |
| hostage | gerowgān | گروگان |

| to swindle (deceive) | farib dādan | فریب دادن |
| swindle, deception | farib | فریب |
| swindler | hoqqe bāz | حقه باز |

| to bribe (vt) | rešve dādan | رشوه دادن |
| bribery | rešve | رشوه |
| bribe | rešve | رشوه |

| poison | zahr | زهر |
| to poison (vt) | masmum kardan | مسموم کردن |
| to poison oneself | masmum šodan | مسموم شدن |

| suicide (act) | xod-koši | خودکشی |
| suicide (person) | xod-koši konande | خودکشی کننده |

| | | |
|---|---|---|
| to threaten (vt) | tahdid kardan | تهدید کردن |
| threat | tahdid | تهدید |
| to make an attempt | su'-e qasd kardan | سوء قصد کردن |
| attempt (attack) | su'-e qasd | سوء قصد |
| to steal (a car) | robudan | ربودن |
| to hijack (a plane) | havāpeymā robāyi | هواپیما ربایی |
| revenge | enteqām | انتقام |
| to avenge (get revenge) | enteqām gereftan | انتقام گرفتن |
| to torture (vt) | šekanje dādan | شکنجه دادن |
| torture | šekanje | شکنجه |
| to torment (vt) | aziyat kardan | اذیت کردن |
| pirate | dozd-e daryāyi | دزد دریایی |
| hooligan | owbāš | اوباش |
| armed (adj) | mosallah | مسلح |
| violence | xošunat | خشونت |
| illegal (unlawful) | qeyr-e qānuni | غیر قانونی |
| spying (espionage) | jāsusi | جاسوسی |
| to spy (vi) | jāsusi kardan | جاسوسی کردن |

## 120. Police. Law. Part 1

| | | |
|---|---|---|
| justice | edālat | عدالت |
| court (see you in ~) | dādgāh | دادگاه |
| judge | qāzi | قاضی |
| jurors | hey'at-e monsefe | هیئت منصفه |
| jury trial | hey'at-e monsefe | هیئت منصفه |
| to judge (vt) | mohākeme kardan | محاکمه کردن |
| lawyer, attorney | vakil | وکیل |
| defendant | mottaham | متهم |
| dock | jāygāh-e mottaham | جایگاه متهم |
| charge | ettehām | اتهام |
| accused | mottaham | متهم |
| sentence | hokm | حکم |
| to sentence (vt) | mahkum kardan | محکوم کردن |
| guilty (culprit) | moqasser | مقصر |
| to punish (vt) | mojāzāt kardan | مجازات کردن |
| punishment | mojāzāt | مجازات |
| fine (penalty) | jarime | جریمه |
| life imprisonment | habs-e abad | حبس ابد |

| death penalty | e'dām | اعدام |
| electric chair | sandali-ye barqi | صندلی برقی |
| gallows | čube-ye dār | چوبه دار |

| to execute (vt) | e'dām kardan | اعدام کردن |
| execution | e'dām | اعدام |

| prison, jail | zendān | زندان |
| cell | sellul-e zendān | سلول زندان |

| escort | eskort | اسکورت |
| prison guard | negahbān zendān | نگهبان زندان |
| prisoner | zendāni | زندانی |

| handcuffs | dastband | دستبند |
| to handcuff (vt) | dastband zadan | دستبند زدن |

| prison break | farār | فرار |
| to break out (vi) | farār kardan | فرار کردن |
| to disappear (vi) | nāpadid šodan | ناپدید شدن |
| to release (from prison) | āzād kardan | آزاد کردن |
| amnesty | afv-e omumi | عفو عمومی |

| police | polis | پلیس |
| police officer | polis | پلیس |
| police station | kalāntari | کلانتری |
| billy club | bātum | باتوم |
| bullhorn | bolandgu | بلندگو |

| patrol car | māšin-e gašt | ماشین گشت |
| siren | āžir-e xatar | آژیر خطر |
| to turn on the siren | āžir rā rowšan kardan | آژیررا روشن کردن |
| siren call | sedā-ye āžir | صدای آژیر |

| crime scene | mahall-e jenāyat | محل جنایت |
| witness | šāhed | شاهد |
| freedom | āzādi | آزادی |
| accomplice | hamdast | همدست |
| to flee (vi) | maxfi šodan | مخفی شدن |
| trace (to leave a ~) | rad | رد |

## 121. Police. Law. Part 2

| search (investigation) | jostoju | جستجو |
| to look for ... | jostoju kardan | جستجو کردن |
| suspicion | šok | شک |
| suspicious (e.g., ~ vehicle) | maškuk | مشکوک |
| to stop (cause to halt) | motevaghef kardan | متوقف کردن |
| to detain (keep in custody) | dastgir kardan | دستگیر کردن |
| case (lawsuit) | parvande | پرونده |

| investigation | tahqiq | تحقیق |
| detective | kārāgāh | کارآگاه |
| investigator | bāzpors | بازپرس |
| hypothesis | farziye | فرضیه |

| motive | angize | انگیزه |
| interrogation | bāzporsi | بازپرسی |
| to interrogate (vt) | bāzporsi kardan | بازپرسی کردن |
| to question | estentāq kardan | استنطاق کردن |
| (~ neighbors, etc.) | | |
| check (identity ~) | taftiš | تفتیش |

| round-up | mohāsere | محاصره |
| search (~ warrant) | taftiš | تفتیش |
| chase (pursuit) | ta'qib | تعقیب |
| to pursue, to chase | ta'qib kardan | تعقیب کردن |
| to track (a criminal) | donbāl kardan | دنبال کردن |

| arrest | bāzdāšt | بازداشت |
| to arrest (sb) | bāzdāšt kardan | بازداشت کردن |
| to catch (thief, etc.) | dastgir kardan | دستگیر کردن |
| capture | dastgiri | دستگیری |

| document | sanad | سند |
| proof (evidence) | esbāt | اثبات |
| to prove (vt) | esbāt kardan | اثبات کردن |
| footprint | rad-e pā | رد پا |
| fingerprints | asar-e angošt | اثر انگشت |
| piece of evidence | šavāhed | شواهد |

| alibi | ozr-e qeybat | عذر غیبت |
| innocent (not guilty) | bi gonāh | بی گناه |
| injustice | bi edālati | بی عدالتی |
| unjust, unfair (adj) | qeyr-e ādelāne | غیر عادلانه |

| criminal (adj) | jenāyi | جنایی |
| to confiscate (vt) | mosādere kardan | مصادره کردن |
| drug (illegal substance) | mavādd-e moxadder | مواد مخدر |
| weapon, gun | selāh | سلاح |
| to disarm (vt) | xal'-e selāh kardan | خلع سلاح کردن |
| to order (command) | farmān dādan | فرمان دادن |
| to disappear (vi) | nāpadid šodan | ناپدید شدن |

| law | qānun | قانون |
| legal, lawful (adj) | qānuni | قانونی |
| illegal, illicit (adj) | qeyr-e qānuni | غیر قانونی |

| responsibility (blame) | mas'uliyat | مسئولیت |
| responsible (adj) | mas'ul | مسئول |

# NATURE

## The Earth. Part 1

### 122. Outer space

| space | fazā | فضا |
| space (as adj) | fazāyi | فضایی |
| outer space | fazā-ye keyhān | فضای کیهان |
| world | jahān | جهان |
| universe | giti | گیتی |
| galaxy | kahkešān | کهکشان |
| star | setāre | ستاره |
| constellation | surat-e falaki | صورت فلکی |
| planet | sayyāre | سیاره |
| satellite | māhvāre | ماهواره |
| meteorite | sang-e āsmāni | سنگ آسمانی |
| comet | setāre-ye donbāle dār | ستارۀ دنباله دار |
| asteroid | šahāb | شهاب |
| orbit | madār | مدار |
| to revolve (~ around the Earth) | gardidan | گردیدن |
| atmosphere | jav | جو |
| the Sun | āftāb | آفتاب |
| solar system | manzume-ye šamsi | منظومه شمسی |
| solar eclipse | kosuf | کسوف |
| the Earth | zamin | زمین |
| the Moon | māh | ماه |
| Mars | merrix | مریخ |
| Venus | zahre | زهره |
| Jupiter | moštari | مشتری |
| Saturn | zohal | زحل |
| Mercury | atārod | عطارد |
| Uranus | orānus | اورانوس |
| Neptune | nepton | نپتون |
| Pluto | poloton | پلوتون |
| Milky Way | kahkešān rāh-e širi | کهکشان راه شیری |

| Great Bear (Ursa Major) | dobb-e akbar | دب اکبر |
| North Star | setāre-ye qotbi | ستاره قطبی |

| Martian | merrixi | مریخی |
| extraterrestrial (n) | farā zamini | فرا زمینی |
| alien | mowjud fazāyi | موجود فضایی |
| flying saucer | bošqāb-e parande | بشقاب پرنده |

| spaceship | fazā peymā | فضا پیما |
| space station | istgāh-e fazāyi | ایستگاه فضایی |
| blast-off | rāh andāzi | راه اندازی |

| engine | motor | موتور |
| nozzle | nāzel | نازل |
| fuel | suxt | سوخت |

| cockpit, flight deck | kābin | کابین |
| antenna | ānten | آنتن |
| porthole | panjere | پنجره |
| solar panel | bātri-ye xoršidi | باطری خورشیدی |
| spacesuit | lebās-e fazānavardi | لباس فضانوردی |

| weightlessness | bi vazni | بی وزنی |
| oxygen | oksižen | اکسیژن |

| docking (in space) | vasl | وصل |
| to dock (vi, vt) | vasl kardan | وصل کردن |

| observatory | rasadxāne | رصدخانه |
| telescope | teleskop | تلسکوپ |
| to observe (vt) | mošāhede kardan | مشاهده کردن |
| to explore (vt) | kašf kardan | کشف کردن |

## 123. The Earth

| the Earth | zamin | زمین |
| the globe (the Earth) | kare-ye zamin | کرۀ زمین |
| planet | sayyāre | سیاره |

| atmosphere | jav | جو |
| geography | joqrāfiyā | جغرافیا |
| nature | tabi'at | طبیعت |

| globe (table ~) | kare-ye joqrāfiyāyi | کرۀ جغرافیایی |
| map | naqše | نقشه |
| atlas | atlas | اطلس |

| Europe | orupā | اروپا |
| Asia | āsiyā | آسیا |
| Africa | āfriqā | آفریقا |

| Australia | ostorāliyā | استرالیا |
| America | emrikā | امریکا |
| North America | emrikā-ye šomāli | امریکای شمالی |
| South America | emrikā-ye jonubi | امریکای جنوبی |

| Antarctica | qotb-e jonub | قطب جنوب |
| the Arctic | qotb-e šomāl | قطب شمال |

## 124. Cardinal directions

| north | šomāl | شمال |
| to the north | be šomāl | به شمال |
| in the north | dar šomāl | در شمال |
| northern (adj) | šomāli | شمالی |

| south | jonub | جنوب |
| to the south | be jonub | به جنوب |
| in the south | dar jonub | در جنوب |
| southern (adj) | jonubi | جنوبی |

| west | qarb | غرب |
| to the west | be qarb | به غرب |
| in the west | dar qarb | در غرب |
| western (adj) | qarbi | غربی |

| east | šarq | شرق |
| to the east | be šarq | به شرق |
| in the east | dar šarq | در شرق |
| eastern (adj) | šarqi | شرقی |

## 125. Sea. Ocean

| sea | daryā | دریا |
| ocean | oqyānus | اقیانوس |
| gulf (bay) | xalij | خلیج |
| straits | tange | تنگه |

| land (solid ground) | zamin | زمین |
| continent (mainland) | qāre | قاره |

| island | jazire | جزیره |
| peninsula | šeb-e jazire | شبه جزیره |
| archipelago | majma'-ol-jazāyer | مجمع‌الجزایر |

| bay, cove | xalij-e kučak | خلیج کوچک |
| harbor | langargāh | لنگرگاه |
| lagoon | mordāb | مرداب |
| cape | damāqe | دماغه |

137

| atoll | jazire-ye marjāni | جزیره مرجانی |
| reef | tappe-ye daryāyi | تپه دریایی |
| coral | marjān | مرجان |
| coral reef | tappe-ye marjāni | تپه مرجانی |

| deep (adj) | amiq | عمیق |
| depth (deep water) | omq | عمق |
| abyss | partgāh | پرتگاه |
| trench (e.g., Mariana ~) | derāz godāl | درازگودال |
| current (Ocean ~) | jaryān | جریان |
| to surround (bathe) | ehāte kardan | احاطه کردن |

| shore | sāhel | ساحل |
| coast | sāhel | ساحل |

| flow (flood tide) | mod | مد |
| ebb (ebb tide) | jazr | جزر |
| shoal | sāhel-e šeni | ساحل شنی |
| bottom (~ of the sea) | qa'r | قعر |

| wave | mowj | موج |
| crest (~ of a wave) | nok | نوک |
| spume (sea foam) | kaf | کف |
| storm (sea storm) | tufān-e daryāyi | طوفان دریایی |
| hurricane | tufān | طوفان |
| tsunami | sonāmi | سونامی |
| calm (dead ~) | sokun-e daryā | سکون دریا |
| quiet, calm (adj) | ārām | آرام |

| pole | qotb | قطب |
| polar (adj) | qotbi | قطبی |

| latitude | arz-e joqrāfiyāyi | عرض جغرافیایی |
| longitude | tul-e joqrāfiyāyi | طول جغرافیایی |
| parallel | movāzi | موازی |
| equator | xatt-e ostavā | خط استوا |

| sky | āsemān | آسمان |
| horizon | ofoq | افق |
| air | havā | هوا |

| lighthouse | fānus-e daryāyi | فانوس دریایی |
| to dive (vi) | širje raftan | شیرجه رفتن |
| to sink (ab. boat) | qarq šodan | غرق شدن |
| treasures | ganj | گنج |

## 126. Seas' and Oceans' names

| Atlantic Ocean | oqyānus-e atlas | اقیانوس اطلس |
| Indian Ocean | oqyānus-e hend | اقیانوس هند |

| Pacific Ocean | oqyānus-e ārām | اقیانوس آرام |
| Arctic Ocean | oqyānus-e monjamed-e šomāli | اقیانوس منجمد شمالی |

| Black Sea | daryā-ye siyāh | دریای سیاه |
| Red Sea | daryā-ye sorx | دریای سرخ |
| Yellow Sea | daryā-ye zard | دریای زرد |
| White Sea | daryā-ye sefid | دریای سفید |

| Caspian Sea | daryā-ye xazar | دریای خزر |
| Dead Sea | daryā-ye morde | دریای مرده |
| Mediterranean Sea | daryā-ye meditarāne | دریای مدیترانه |

| Aegean Sea | daryā-ye eže | دریای اژه |
| Adriatic Sea | daryā-ye ādriyātik | دریای آدریاتیک |

| Arabian Sea | daryā-ye arab | دریای عرب |
| Sea of Japan | daryā-ye žāpon | دریای ژاپن |
| Bering Sea | daryā-ye brinq | دریای برینگ |
| South China Sea | daryā-ye čin-e jonubi | دریای چین جنوبی |

| Coral Sea | daryā-ye marjān | دریای مرجان |
| Tasman Sea | daryā-ye tās-emān | دریای تاسمان |
| Caribbean Sea | daryā-ye kārāib | دریای کارائیب |

| Barents Sea | daryā-ye barntz | دریای بارنتز |
| Kara Sea | daryā-ye kārā | دریای کارا |

| North Sea | daryā-ye šomāl | دریای شمال |
| Baltic Sea | daryā-ye bāltik | دریای بالتیک |
| Norwegian Sea | daryā-ye norvež | دریای نروژ |

## 127. Mountains

| mountain | kuh | کوه |
| mountain range | rešte-ye kuh | رشته کوه |
| mountain ridge | selsele-ye jebāl | سلسله جبال |

| summit, top | qolle | قله |
| peak | qolle | قله |
| foot (~ of the mountain) | dāmane-ye kuh | دامنه کوه |
| slope (mountainside) | šib | شیب |

| volcano | ātaš-fešān | آتشفشان |
| active volcano | ātaš-fešān-e fa'āl | آتش فشان فعال |
| dormant volcano | ātaš-fešān-e xāmuš | آتش فشان خاموش |

| eruption | favarān | فوران |
| crater | dahāne-ye ātašfešān | دهانه آتش فشان |
| magma | māgmā | ماگما |

139

| lava | godāze | گدازه |
| molten (~ lava) | godāxte | گداخته |

| canyon | tange | تنگه |
| gorge | darre-ye tang | دره تنگ |
| crevice | tange | تنگه |
| abyss (chasm) | partgāh | پرتگاه |

| pass, col | gozargāh | گذرگاه |
| plateau | falāt | فلات |
| cliff | saxre | صخره |
| hill | tappe | تپه |

| glacier | yaxčāl | یخچال |
| waterfall | ābšār | آبشار |
| geyser | češme-ye āb-e garm | چشمهٔ آب گرم |
| lake | daryāče | دریاچه |

| plain | jolge | جلگه |
| landscape | manzare | منظره |
| echo | en'ekās-e sowt | انعکاس صوت |

| alpinist | kuhnavard | کوهنورد |
| rock climber | saxre-ye navard | صخره نورد |
| to conquer (in climbing) | fath kardan | فتح کردن |
| climb (an easy ~) | so'ud | صعود |

## 128. Mountains names

| The Alps | ālp | آلپ |
| Mont Blanc | moan belān | مون بلان |
| The Pyrenees | pirene | پیرنه |

| The Carpathians | kuhhā-ye kārpāt | کوههای کارپات |
| The Ural Mountains | kuhe-i orāl | کوههای اورال |

| The Caucasus Mountains | qafqāz | قفقاز |
| Mount Elbrus | alborz | البرز |

| The Altai Mountains | āltāy | آلتای |
| The Tian Shan | tiyān šān | تیان شان |
| The Pamir Mountains | pāmir | پامیر |

| The Himalayas | himāliyā-vo | هیمالیا |
| Mount Everest | everest | اورست |

| The Andes | ānd | آند |
| Mount Kilimanjaro | kelimānjāro | کلیمانجارو |

## 129. Rivers

| river | rudxāne | رودخانه |
|---|---|---|
| spring (natural source) | češme | چشمه |
| riverbed (river channel) | bastar | بستر |
| basin (river valley) | howze | حوضه |
| to flow into ... | rixtan | ریختن |

| tributary | enše'āb | انشعاب |
|---|---|---|
| bank (of river) | sāhel | ساحل |

| current (stream) | jaryān | جریان |
|---|---|---|
| downstream (adv) | be samt-e pāin-e rudxāne | به سمت پائین رودخانه |
| upstream (adv) | be samt-e bālā-ye rudxāne | به سمت بالای رودخانه |

| inundation | seyl | سیل |
|---|---|---|
| flooding | toqyān | طغیان |
| to overflow (vi) | toqyān kardan | طغیان کردن |
| to flood (vt) | toqyān kardan | طغیان کردن |

| shallow (shoal) | tangāb | تنگاب |
|---|---|---|
| rapids | tondāb | تندآب |

| dam | sad | سد |
|---|---|---|
| canal | kānāl | کانال |
| reservoir (artificial lake) | maxzan-e āb | مخزن آب |
| sluice, lock | ābgir | آبگیر |

| water body (pond, etc.) | maxzan-e āb | مخزن آب |
|---|---|---|
| swamp (marshland) | bātlāq | باتلاق |
| bog, marsh | lajan zār | لجن زار |
| whirlpool | gerdāb | گرداب |

| stream (brook) | ravad | رود |
|---|---|---|
| drinking (ab. water) | āšāmidani | آشامیدنی |
| fresh (~ water) | širin | شیرین |

| ice | yax | یخ |
|---|---|---|
| to freeze over (ab. river, etc.) | yax bastan | یخ بستن |

## 130. Rivers' names

| Seine | sen | سن |
|---|---|---|
| Loire | lavār | لوآر |

| Thames | timz | تیمز |
|---|---|---|
| Rhine | rāyn | راین |
| Danube | dānub | دانوب |

| Volga | volgā | ولگا |
| Don | don | دن |
| Lena | lenā | لنا |

| Yellow River | rud-e zard | رود زرد |
| Yangtze | yāng tese | یانگ تسه |
| Mekong | mekung | مکونگ |
| Ganges | gong | گنگ |

| Nile River | neyl | نیل |
| Congo River | kongo | کنگو |
| Okavango River | okavango | اوکاوانگو |
| Zambezi River | zāmbezi | زامبزی |
| Limpopo River | rud-e limpupu | رود لیمپوپو |
| Mississippi River | mi si si pi | می سی سی پی |

## 131. Forest

| forest, wood | jangal | جنگل |
| forest (as adj) | jangali | جنگلی |

| thick forest | jangal-e anbuh | جنگل انبوه |
| grove | biše | بیشه |
| forest clearing | marqzār | مرغزار |

| thicket | biše-hā | بیشه ها |
| scrubland | bute zār | بوته زار |

| footpath (troddenpath) | kure-ye rāh | کوره راه |
| gully | darre | دره |

| tree | deraxt | درخت |
| leaf | barg | برگ |
| leaves (foliage) | šāx-o barg | شاخ و برگ |

| fall of leaves | barg rizi | برگ ریزی |
| to fall (ab. leaves) | rixtan | ریختن |
| top (of the tree) | nok | نوک |

| branch | šāxe | شاخه |
| bough | šāxe | شاخه |
| bud (on shrub, tree) | šokufe | شکوفه |
| needle (of pine tree) | suzan | سوزن |
| pine cone | maxrut-e kāj | مخروط کاج |

| hollow (in a tree) | surāx | سوراخ |
| nest | lāne | لانه |
| burrow (animal hole) | lāne | لانه |
| trunk | tane | تنه |
| root | riše | ریشه |

| | | |
|---|---|---|
| bark | pust | پوست |
| moss | xaze | خزه |
| to uproot (remove trees or tree stumps) | rišekan kardan | ریشه کن کردن |
| to chop down | boridan | بریدن |
| to deforest (vt) | boridan | بریدن |
| tree stump | kande-ye deraxt | کندهٔ درخت |
| campfire | ātaš | آتش |
| forest fire | ātaš suzi | آتش سوزی |
| to extinguish (vt) | xāmuš kardan | خاموش کردن |
| forest ranger | jangal bān | جنگل بان |
| protection | mohāfezat | محافظت |
| to protect (~ nature) | mohāfezat kardan | محافظت کردن |
| poacher | šekārči-ye qeyr-e qānuni | شکارچی غیر قانونی |
| steel trap | tale | تله |
| to gather, to pick (vt) | čidan | چیدن |
| to lose one's way | gom šodan | گم شدن |

## 132. Natural resources

| | | |
|---|---|---|
| natural resources | manābe-'e tabii | منابع طبیعی |
| minerals | mavādd-e ma'dani | مواد معدنی |
| deposits | tah nešast | ته نشست |
| field (e.g., oilfield) | meydān | میدان |
| to mine (extract) | estexrāj kardan | استخراج کردن |
| mining (extraction) | estexrāj | استخراج |
| ore | sang-e ma'dani | سنگ معدنی |
| mine (e.g., for coal) | ma'dan | معدن |
| shaft (mine ~) | ma'dan | معدن |
| miner | ma'danči | معدنچی |
| gas (natural ~) | gāz | گاز |
| gas pipeline | lule-ye gāz | لولهٔ گاز |
| oil (petroleum) | naft | نفت |
| oil pipeline | lule-ye naft | لولهٔ نفت |
| oil well | čāh-e naft | چاه نفت |
| derrick (tower) | dakal-e haffāri | دکل حفاری |
| tanker | tānker | تانکر |
| sand | šen | شن |
| limestone | sang-e āhak | سنگ آهک |
| gravel | sangrize | سنگریزه |
| peat | turb | تورب |
| clay | xāk-e ros | خاک رس |

| coal | zoqāl sang | زغال سنگ |
| iron (ore) | āhan | آهن |
| gold | talā | طلا |
| silver | noqre | نقره |
| nickel | nikel | نیکل |
| copper | mes | مس |
| zinc | ruy | روی |
| manganese | mangenez | منگنز |
| mercury | jive | جیوه |
| lead | sorb | سرب |
| mineral | mādde-ye ma'dani | مادۀ معدنی |
| crystal | bolur | بلور |
| marble | marmar | مرمر |
| uranium | orāniyom | اورانیوم |

# The Earth. Part 2

## 133. Weather

| | | |
|---|---|---|
| weather | havā | هوا |
| weather forecast | piš bini havā | پیش بینی هوا |
| temperature | damā | دما |
| thermometer | damāsanj | دماسنج |
| barometer | havāsanj | هواسنج |
| | | |
| humid (adj) | martub | مرطوب |
| humidity | rotubat | رطوبت |
| | | |
| heat (extreme ~) | garmā | گرما |
| hot (torrid) | dāq | داغ |
| it's hot | havā xeyli garm ast | هوا خیلی گرم است |
| | | |
| it's warm | havā garm ast | هوا گرم است |
| warm (moderately hot) | garm | گرم |
| | | |
| it's cold | sard ast | سرد است |
| cold (adj) | sard | سرد |
| | | |
| sun | āftāb | آفتاب |
| to shine (vi) | tābidan | تابیدن |
| sunny (day) | āftābi | آفتابی |
| to come up (vi) | tolu' kardan | طلوع کردن |
| to set (vi) | qorob kardan | غروب کردن |
| | | |
| cloud | abr | ابر |
| cloudy (adj) | abri | ابری |
| rain cloud | abr-e bārānzā | ابر باران زا |
| somber (gloomy) | tire | تیره |
| | | |
| rain | bārān | باران |
| it's raining | bārān mibārad | باران می بارد |
| rainy (~ day, weather) | bārāni | بارانی |
| to drizzle (vi) | nam-nam bāridan | نم نم باریدن |
| | | |
| pouring rain | bārān šodid | باران شدید |
| downpour | ragbār | رگبار |
| heavy (e.g., ~ rain) | šadid | شدید |
| puddle | čāle | چاله |
| to get wet (in rain) | xis šodan | خیس شدن |
| fog (mist) | meh | مه |
| foggy | meh ālud | مه آلود |

| snow | barf | برف |
|------|------|-----|
| it's snowing | barf mibārad | برف می بارد |

## 134. Severe weather. Natural disasters

| thunderstorm | tufān | طوفان |
|------|------|-----|
| lightning (~ strike) | barq | برق |
| to flash (vi) | barq zadan | برق زدن |

| thunder | ra'd | رعد |
|------|------|-----|
| to thunder (vi) | qorridan | غریدن |
| it's thundering | ra'd mizanad | رعد می زند |

| hail | tagarg | تگرگ |
|------|------|-----|
| it's hailing | tagarg mibārad | تگرگ می بارد |

| to flood (vt) | toqyān kardan | طغیان کردن |
|------|------|-----|
| flood, inundation | seyl | سیل |

| earthquake | zamin-larze | زمین لرزه |
|------|------|-----|
| tremor, quake | tekān | تکان |
| epicenter | kānun-e zaminlarze | کانون زمین لرزه |

| eruption | favarān | فوران |
|------|------|-----|
| lava | godāze | گدازه |

| twister, tornado | gerdbād | گردباد |
|------|------|-----|
| typhoon | tufān | طوفان |

| hurricane | tufān | طوفان |
|------|------|-----|
| storm | tufān | طوفان |
| tsunami | sonāmi | سونامی |

| cyclone | gerdbād | گردباد |
|------|------|-----|
| bad weather | havā-ye bad | هوای بد |
| fire (accident) | ātaš suzi | آتش سوزی |
| disaster | balā-ye tabi'i | بلای طبیعی |
| meteorite | sang-e āsmāni | سنگ آسمانی |

| avalanche | bahman | بهمن |
|------|------|-----|
| snowslide | bahman | بهمن |
| blizzard | kulāk | کولاک |
| snowstorm | barf-o burān | برف و بوران |

# Fauna

## 135. Mammals. Predators

| | | |
|---|---|---|
| predator | heyvān-e darande | حیوان درنده |
| tiger | bebar | ببر |
| lion | šir | شیر |
| wolf | gorg | گرگ |
| fox | rubāh | روباه |
| | | |
| jaguar | jagvār | جگوار |
| leopard | palang | پلنگ |
| cheetah | yuzpalang | یوزپلنگ |
| | | |
| black panther | palang-e siyāh | پلنگ سیاه |
| puma | yuzpalang | یوزپلنگ |
| snow leopard | palang-e barfi | پلنگ برفی |
| lynx | siyāh guš | سیاه گوش |
| | | |
| coyote | gorg-e sahrāyi | گرگ صحرایی |
| jackal | šoqāl | شغال |
| hyena | kaftār | کفتار |

## 136. Wild animals

| | | |
|---|---|---|
| animal | heyvān | حیوان |
| beast (animal) | heyvān | حیوان |
| | | |
| squirrel | sanjāb | سنجاب |
| hedgehog | xārpošt | خارپشت |
| hare | xarguš | خرگوش |
| rabbit | xarguš | خرگوش |
| | | |
| badger | gurkan | گورکن |
| raccoon | rākon | راکون |
| hamster | muš-e bozorg | موش بزرگ |
| marmot | muš-e xormā-ye kuhi | موش خرمای کوهی |
| | | |
| mole | muš-e kur | موش کور |
| mouse | muš | موش |
| rat | muš-e sahrāyi | موش صحرایی |
| bat | xoffāš | خفاش |
| ermine | qāqom | قاقم |
| sable | samur | سمور |

| marten | samur | سمور |
| weasel | rāsu | راسو |
| mink | tire-ye rāsu | تیره راسو |

| beaver | sag-e ābi | سگ آبی |
| otter | samur ābi | سمور آبی |

| horse | asb | اسب |
| moose | gavazn | گوزن |
| deer | āhu | آهو |
| camel | šotor | شتر |

| bison | gāvmiš | گاومیش |
| aurochs | gāv miš | گاو میش |
| buffalo | bufālo | بوفالو |

| zebra | gurexar | گورخر |
| antelope | boz-e kuhi | بز کوهی |
| roe deer | šukā | شوکا |
| fallow deer | qazāl | غزال |
| chamois | boz-e kuhi | بز کوهی |
| wild boar | gorāz | گراز |

| whale | nahang | نهنگ |
| seal | fak | فک |
| walrus | širmāhi | شیرماهی |
| fur seal | gorbe-ye ābi | گربۀ آبی |
| dolphin | delfin | دلفین |

| bear | xers | خرس |
| polar bear | xers-e sefid | خرس سفید |
| panda | pāndā | پاندا |

| monkey | meymun | میمون |
| chimpanzee | šampānze | شمپانزه |
| orangutan | orāngutān | اورانگوتان |
| gorilla | guril | گوریل |
| macaque | mākāk | ماکاک |
| gibbon | gibon | گیبون |

| elephant | fil | فیل |
| rhinoceros | kargadan | کرگدن |
| giraffe | zarrāfe | زرافه |
| hippopotamus | asb-e ābi | اسب آبی |

| kangaroo | kāngoro | کانگورو |
| koala (bear) | kovālā | کوالا |

| mongoose | xadang | خدنگ |
| chinchilla | čin čila | چین چیلا |
| skunk | rāsu-ye badbu | راسوی بدبو |
| porcupine | taši | تشی |

## 137. Domestic animals

| cat | gorbe | گربه |
| tomcat | gorbe-ye nar | گربهٔ نر |
| dog | sag | سگ |

| horse | asb | اسب |
| stallion (male horse) | asb-e nar | اسب نر |
| mare | mādiyān | مادیان |

| cow | gāv | گاو |
| bull | gāv-e nar | گاو نر |
| ox | gāv-e axte | گاو اخته |

| sheep (ewe) | gusfand | گوسفند |
| ram | gusfand-e nar | گوسفند نر |
| goat | boz-e mādde | بز ماده |
| billy goat, he-goat | boz-e nar | بز نر |

| donkey | xar | خر |
| mule | qāter | قاطر |

| pig, hog | xuk | خوک |
| piglet | bače-ye xuk | بچهٔ خوک |
| rabbit | xarguš | خرگوش |

| hen (chicken) | morq | مرغ |
| rooster | xorus | خروس |

| duck | ordak | اردک |
| drake | ordak-e nar | اردک نر |
| goose | qāz | غاز |

| tom turkey, gobbler | buqalamun-e nar | بوقلمون نر |
| turkey (hen) | buqalamun-e māde | بوقلمون ماده |

| domestic animals | heyvānāt-e ahli | حیوانات اهلی |
| tame (e.g., ~ hamster) | ahli | اهلی |
| to tame (vt) | rām kardan | رام کردن |
| to breed (vt) | parvareš dādan | پرورش دادن |

| farm | mazrae | مزرعه |
| poultry | morq-e xānegi | مرغ خانگی |
| cattle | dām | دام |
| herd (cattle) | galle | گله |

| stable | establ | اصطبل |
| pigpen | āqol xuk | آغل خوک |
| cowshed | āqol gāv | آغل گاو |
| rabbit hutch | lanye xarguš | لانه خرگوش |
| hen house | morq dāni | مرغ دانی |

## 138. Birds

| bird | parande | پرنده |
| pigeon | kabutar | کبوتر |
| sparrow | gonješk | گنجشک |
| tit (great tit) | morq-e zanburxār | مرغ زنبورخوار |
| magpie | zāqi | زاغی |

| raven | kalāq-e siyāh | کلاغ سیاه |
| crow | kalāq | کلاغ |
| jackdaw | zāq | زاغ |
| rook | kalāq-e siyāh | کلاغ سیاه |

| duck | ordak | اردک |
| goose | qāz | غاز |
| pheasant | qarqāvol | قرقاول |

| eagle | oqāb | عقاب |
| hawk | qerqi | قرقی |
| falcon | šāhin | شاهین |
| vulture | karkas | کرکس |
| condor (Andean ~) | karkas-e emrikāyi | کرکس امریکایی |

| swan | qu | قو |
| crane | dornā | درنا |
| stork | lak lak | لک لک |

| parrot | tuti | طوطی |
| hummingbird | morq-e magas-e xār | مرغ مگس خوار |
| peacock | tāvus | طاووس |

| ostrich | šotormorq | شترمرغ |
| heron | havāsil | حواصیل |
| flamingo | felāmingo | فلامینگو |
| pelican | pelikān | پلیکان |

| nightingale | bolbol | بلبل |
| swallow | parastu | پرستو |

| thrush | bāstarak | باسترک |
| song thrush | torqe | طرقه |
| blackbird | tukā-ye siyāh | توکای سیاه |

| swift | bādxorak | بادخورک |
| lark | čakāvak | چکاوک |
| quail | belderčin | بلدرچین |

| woodpecker | dārkub | دارکوب |
| cuckoo | fāxte | فاخته |
| owl | joqd | جغد |
| eagle owl | šāh buf | شاه بوف |

| | | |
|---|---|---|
| wood grouse | siāh xorus | سیاه خروس |
| black grouse | siāh xorus-e jangali | سیاه خروس جنگلی |
| partridge | kabk | کبک |
| | | |
| starling | sār | سار |
| canary | qanāri | قناری |
| hazel grouse | siyāh xorus-e fandoqi | سیاه خروس فندقی |
| chaffinch | sehre-ye jangali | سهره جنگلی |
| bullfinch | sohre sar-e siyāh | سهره سر سیاه |
| | | |
| seagull | morq-e daryāyi | مرغ دریایی |
| albatross | morq-e daryāyi | مرغ دریایی |
| penguin | pangoan | پنگوئن |

## 139. Fish. Marine animals

| | | |
|---|---|---|
| bream | māhi-ye sim | ماهی سیم |
| carp | kapur | کپور |
| perch | māhi-e luti | ماهی لوتی |
| catfish | gorbe-ye māhi | گربه ماهی |
| pike | ordak māhi | اردک ماهی |
| | | |
| salmon | māhi-ye salemon | ماهی سالمون |
| sturgeon | māhi-ye xāviār | ماهی خاویار |
| | | |
| herring | māhi-ye šur | ماهی شور |
| Atlantic salmon | sālmon-e atlāntik | سالمون اتلانتیک |
| mackerel | māhi-ye esqumeri | ماهی اسقومری |
| flatfish | sofre māhi | سفره ماهی |
| | | |
| zander, pike perch | suf | سوف |
| cod | māhi-ye rowqan | ماهی روغن |
| tuna | tan māhi | تن ماهی |
| trout | māhi-ye qezelālā | ماهی قزل آلا |
| | | |
| eel | mārmāhi | مارماهی |
| electric ray | partomahiye barqi | پرتوماهی برقی |
| moray eel | mārmāhi | مارماهی |
| piranha | pirānā | پیرانا |
| | | |
| shark | kuse-ye māhi | کوسه ماهی |
| dolphin | delfin | دلفین |
| whale | nahang | نهنگ |
| | | |
| crab | xarčang | خرچنگ |
| jellyfish | arus-e daryāyi | عروس دریایی |
| octopus | hašt pā | هشت پا |
| | | |
| starfish | setāre-ye daryāyi | ستاره دریایی |
| sea urchin | xārpošt-e daryāyi | خارپشت دریایی |

| seahorse | asb-e daryāyi | اسب دریایی |
| oyster | sadaf-e xorāki | صدف خوراکی |
| shrimp | meygu | میگو |
| lobster | xarčang-e daryāyi | خرچنگ دریایی |
| spiny lobster | xarčang-e xārdār | خرچنگ خاردار |

## 140. Amphibians. Reptiles

| snake | mār | مار |
| venomous (snake) | sammi | سمی |

| viper | af'i | افعی |
| cobra | kobrā | کبرا |
| python | mār-e pinton | مار پیتون |
| boa | mār-e bwa | مار بوا |

| grass snake | mār-e čaman | مار چمن |
| rattle snake | mār-e zangi | مار زنگی |
| anaconda | mār-e ānākondā | مار آناکوندا |

| lizard | susmār | سوسمار |
| iguana | susmār-e deraxti | سوسمار درختی |
| monitor lizard | bozmajje | بزمجه |
| salamander | samandar | سمندر |
| chameleon | āftāb-parast | آفتاب پرست |
| scorpion | aqrab | عقرب |

| turtle | lāk pošt | لاک پشت |
| frog | qurbāqe | قورباغه |
| toad | vazaq | وزغ |
| crocodile | temsāh | تمساح |

## 141. Insects

| insect, bug | hašare | حشره |
| butterfly | parvāne | پروانه |
| ant | murče | مورچه |
| fly | magas | مگس |
| mosquito | paše | پشه |
| beetle | susk | سوسک |

| wasp | zanbur | زنبور |
| bee | zanbur-e asal | زنبور عسل |
| bumblebee | xar zanbur | خرزنبور |
| gadfly (botfly) | xarmagas | خرمگس |

| spider | ankabut | عنکبوت |
| spiderweb | tār-e ankabut | تارعنکبوت |

| | | |
|---|---|---|
| dragonfly | sanjāqak | سنجاقک |
| grasshopper | malax | ملخ |
| moth (night butterfly) | bid | بید |
| | | |
| cockroach | susk | سوسک |
| tick | kane | کنه |
| flea | kak | کک |
| midge | paše-ye rize | پشه ریزه |
| | | |
| locust | malax | ملخ |
| snail | halazun | حلزون |
| cricket | jirjirak | جیرجیرک |
| lightning bug | kerm-e šab-tāb | کرم شب تاب |
| ladybug | kafšduzak | کفشدوزک |
| cockchafer | susk bāldār | سوسک بالدار |
| | | |
| leech | zālu | زالو |
| caterpillar | kerm-e abrišam | کرم ابریشم |
| earthworm | kerm | کرم |
| larva | lārv | لارو |

# Flora

## 142. Trees

| | | |
|---|---|---|
| tree | deraxt | درخت |
| deciduous (adj) | barg riz | برگ ریز |
| coniferous (adj) | maxrutiyān | مخروطیان |
| evergreen (adj) | hamiše sabz | همیشه سبز |
| | | |
| apple tree | deraxt-e sib | درخت سیب |
| pear tree | golābi | گلابی |
| sweet cherry tree | gilās | گیلاس |
| sour cherry tree | ālbālu | آلبالو |
| plum tree | ālu | آلو |
| | | |
| birch | tus | توس |
| oak | balut | بلوط |
| linden tree | zirfun | زیرفون |
| aspen | senowbar-e larzān | صنوبر لرزان |
| maple | afrā | افرا |
| | | |
| spruce | senowbar | صنوبر |
| pine | kāj | کاج |
| larch | senowbar-e ārāste | صنوبر آراسته |
| fir tree | šāh deraxt | شاه درخت |
| cedar | sedr | سدر |
| | | |
| poplar | sepidār | سپیدار |
| rowan | zabān gonješk-e kuhi | زبان گنجشک کوهی |
| willow | bid | بید |
| alder | tuskā | توسکا |
| | | |
| beech | rāš | راش |
| elm | nārvan-e qermez | نارون قرمز |
| | | |
| ash (tree) | zabān-e gonješk | زبان گنجشک |
| chestnut | šāh balut | شاه بلوط |
| | | |
| magnolia | māgnoliyā | ماگنولیا |
| palm tree | naxl | نخل |
| cypress | sarv | سرو |
| | | |
| mangrove | karnā | کرنا |
| baobab | bāobāb | بائوباب |
| eucalyptus | okaliptus | اوکالیپتوس |
| sequoia | sorx-e čub | سرخ چوب |

## 143. Shrubs

| bush | bute | بوته |
| shrub | bute zār | بوته زار |

| grapevine | angur | انگور |
| vineyard | tākestān | تاکستان |

| raspberry bush | tamešk | تمشک |
| blackcurrant bush | angur-e farangi-ye siyāh | انگور فرنگی سیاه |
| redcurrant bush | angur-e farangi-ye sorx | انگور فرنگی سرخ |
| gooseberry bush | angur-e farangi | انگور فرنگی |

| acacia | aqāqiyā | اقاقیا |
| barberry | zerešk | زرشک |
| jasmine | yāsaman | یاسمن |

| juniper | ardaj | اردج |
| rosebush | bute-ye gol-e mohammadi | بوتۀ گل محمدی |
| dog rose | nastaran | نسترن |

## 144. Fruits. Berries

| fruit | mive | میوه |
| fruits | mive jāt | میوه جات |

| apple | sib | سیب |
| pear | golābi | گلابی |
| plum | ālu | آلو |

| strawberry (garden ~) | tut-e farangi | توت فرنگی |
| sour cherry | ālbālu | آلبالو |
| sweet cherry | gilās | گیلاس |
| grape | angur | انگور |

| raspberry | tamešk | تمشک |
| blackcurrant | angur-e farangi-ye siyāh | انگور فرنگی سیاه |
| redcurrant | angur-e farangi-ye sorx | انگور فرنگی سرخ |
| gooseberry | angur-e farangi | انگور فرنگی |
| cranberry | nārdānak-e vahši | ناردانک وحشی |

| orange | porteqāl | پرتقال |
| mandarin | nārengi | نارنگی |
| pineapple | ānānās | آناناس |
| banana | mowz | موز |
| date | xormā | خرما |

| lemon | limu | لیمو |
| apricot | zardālu | زردآلو |

| peach | holu | هلو |
| kiwi | kivi | کیوی |
| grapefruit | gerip forut | گریپ فوروت |
| | | |
| berry | mive-ye butei | میوهٔ بوته ای |
| berries | mivehā-ye butei | میوه های بوته ای |
| cowberry | tut-e farangi-ye jangali | توت فرنگی جنگلی |
| wild strawberry | zoqāl axte | زغال اخته |
| bilberry | zoqāl axte | زغال اخته |

## 145. Flowers. Plants

| flower | gol | گل |
| bouquet (of flowers) | daste-ye gol | دسته گل |
| | | |
| rose (flower) | gol-e sorx | گل سرخ |
| tulip | lāle | لاله |
| carnation | mixak | میخک |
| gladiolus | susan-e sefid | سوسن سفید |
| | | |
| cornflower | gol-e gandom | گل گندم |
| harebell | gol-e estekāni | گل استکانی |
| dandelion | gol-e qāsedak | گل قاصدک |
| camomile | bābune | بابونه |
| | | |
| aloe | oloviye | آلوئه |
| cactus | kāktus | کاکتوس |
| rubber plant, ficus | fikus | فیکوس |
| | | |
| lily | susan | سوسن |
| geranium | gol-e šam'dāni | گل شمعدانی |
| hyacinth | sonbol | سنبل |
| | | |
| mimosa | mimosā | میموسا |
| narcissus | narges | نرگس |
| nasturtium | gol-e lādan | گل لادن |
| | | |
| orchid | orkide | ارکیده |
| peony | gol-e ašrafi | گل اشرفی |
| violet | banafše | بنفشه |
| | | |
| pansy | banafše-ye farangi | بنفشه فرنگی |
| forget-me-not | gol-e farāmuš-am makon | گل فراموشم مکن |
| daisy | gol-e morvārid | گل مروارید |
| | | |
| poppy | xašxāš | خشخاش |
| hemp | šāh dāne | شاه دانه |
| mint | na'nā' | نعناع |
| lily of the valley | muge | موگه |
| snowdrop | gol-e barfi | گل برفی |

| nettle | gazane | گزنه |
| sorrel | toršak | ترشک |
| water lily | nilufar-e abi | نیلوفر آبی |
| fern | saraxs | سرخس |
| lichen | golesang | گلسنگ |

| greenhouse (tropical ~) | golxāne | گلخانه |
| lawn | čaman | چمن |
| flowerbed | baqče-ye gol | باغچه گل |

| plant | giyāh | گیاه |
| grass | alaf | علف |
| blade of grass | alaf | علف |

| leaf | barg | برگ |
| petal | golbarg | گلبرگ |
| stem | sāqe | ساقه |
| tuber | riše | ریشه |

| young plant (shoot) | javāne | جوانه |
| thorn | xār | خار |

| to blossom (vi) | gol kardan | گل کردن |
| to fade, to wither | pažmorde šodan | پژمرده شدن |
| smell (odor) | bu | بو |
| to cut (flowers) | boridan | بریدن |
| to pick (a flower) | kandan | کندن |

## 146. Cereals, grains

| grain | dāne | دانه |
| cereal crops | qallāt | غلات |
| ear (of barley, etc.) | xuše | خوشه |

| wheat | gandom | گندم |
| rye | čāvdār | چاودار |
| oats | jow-e sahrāyi | جو صحرایی |

| millet | arzan | ارزن |
| barley | jow | جو |

| corn | zorrat | ذرت |
| rice | berenj | برنج |
| buckwheat | gandom-e siyāh | گندم سیاه |

| pea plant | noxod | نخود |
| kidney bean | lubiyā qermez | لوبیا قرمز |
| soy | sowyā | سویا |
| lentil | adas | عدس |
| beans (pulse crops) | lubiyā | لوبیا |

# COUNTRIES. NATIONALITIES

## 147. Western Europe

| Europe | orupā | اروپا |
|---|---|---|
| European Union | ettehādiye-ye orupā | اتحادیه اروپا |
| | | |
| Austria | otriš | اتریش |
| Great Britain | beritāniyā-ye kabir | بریتانیای کبیر |
| England | engelestān | انگلستان |
| Belgium | belžik | بلژیک |
| Germany | ālmān | آلمان |
| | | |
| Netherlands | holand | هلند |
| Holland | holand | هلند |
| Greece | yunān | یونان |
| Denmark | dānmārk | دانمارک |
| Ireland | irland | ایرلند |
| Iceland | island | ایسلند |
| | | |
| Spain | espāniyā | اسپانیا |
| Italy | itāliyā | ایتالیا |
| Cyprus | qebres | قبرس |
| Malta | mālt | مالت |
| | | |
| Norway | norvež | نروژ |
| Portugal | porteqāl | پرتغال |
| Finland | fanlānd | فنلاند |
| France | farānse | فرانسه |
| | | |
| Sweden | sued | سوئد |
| Switzerland | suis | سوئیس |
| Scotland | eskātland | اسکاتلند |
| | | |
| Vatican | vātikān | واتیکان |
| Liechtenstein | lixteneštāyn | لیختن اشتاین |
| Luxembourg | lokzāmborg | لوکزامبورگ |
| Monaco | monāko | موناکو |

## 148. Central and Eastern Europe

| Albania | ālbāni | آلبانی |
|---|---|---|
| Bulgaria | bolqārestān | بلغارستان |
| Hungary | majārestān | مجارستان |

| Latvia | letuni | لتونی |
| Lithuania | litvāni | لیتوانی |
| Poland | lahestān | لهستان |

| Romania | romāni | رومانی |
| Serbia | serbestān | صربستان |
| Slovakia | eslovāki | اسلواکی |

| Croatia | korovāsi | کرواسی |
| Czech Republic | jomhuri-ye ček | جمهوری چک |
| Estonia | estoni | استونی |

| Bosnia and Herzegovina | bosni-yo herzogovin | بوسنی وهرزگوین |
| Macedonia (Republic of ~) | jomhuri-ye maqduniye | جمهوری مقدونیه |
| Slovenia | eslovoni | اسلوونی |
| Montenegro | montenegro | مونتەنگرو |

## 149. Former USSR countries

| Azerbaijan | āzarbāyjān | آذربایجان |
| Armenia | armanestān | ارمنستان |

| Belarus | belārus | بلاروس |
| Georgia | gorjestān | گرجستان |
| Kazakhstan | qazzāqestān | قزاقستان |
| Kirghizia | qerqizestān | قرقیزستان |
| Moldova, Moldavia | moldāvi | مولداوی |

| Russia | rusiye | روسیه |
| Ukraine | okrāyn | اوکراین |

| Tajikistan | tājikestān | تاجیکستان |
| Turkmenistan | torkamanestān | ترکمنستان |
| Uzbekistan | ozbakestān | ازبکستان |

## 150. Asia

| Asia | āsiyā | آسیا |
| Vietnam | viyetnām | ویتنام |
| India | hendustān | هندوستان |
| Israel | esrāil | اسرائیل |

| China | čin | چین |
| Lebanon | lobnān | لبنان |
| Mongolia | moqolestān | مغولستان |

| Malaysia | mālezi | مالزی |
| Pakistan | pākestān | پاکستان |

| Saudi Arabia | arabestān-e so'udi | عربستان سعودی |
| Thailand | tāyland | تایلند |
| Taiwan | tāyvān | تایوان |
| Turkey | torkiye | ترکیه |
| Japan | žāpon | ژاپن |

| Afghanistan | afqānestān | افغانستان |
| Bangladesh | bangelādeš | بنگلادش |
| Indonesia | andonezi | اندونزی |
| Jordan | ordon | اردن |

| Iraq | arāq | عراق |
| Iran | irān | ایران |
| Cambodia | kāmboj | کامبوج |
| Kuwait | koveyt | کویت |

| Laos | lāus | لائوس |
| Myanmar | miyānmār | میانمار |
| Nepal | nepāl | نپال |
| United Arab Emirates | emārāt-e mottahede-ye arabi | امارات متحده عربی |

| Syria | suriye | سوریه |
| Palestine | felestin | فلسطین |
| South Korea | kare-ye jonubi | کرهٔ جنوبی |
| North Korea | kare-ye šomāli | کرهٔ شمالی |

## 151. North America

| United States of America | eyālāt-e mottahede-ye emrikā | ایالات متحدهٔ امریکا |
| Canada | kānādā | کانادا |
| Mexico | mekzik | مکزیک |

## 152. Central and South America

| Argentina | āržāntin | آرژانتین |
| Brazil | berezil | برزیل |
| Colombia | kolombiyā | کلمبیا |
| Cuba | kubā | کوبا |
| Chile | šhili | شیلی |

| Bolivia | bulivi | بولیوی |
| Venezuela | venezuelā | ونزوئلا |
| Paraguay | pārāgue | پاراگوئه |
| Peru | porov | پرو |
| Suriname | surinām | سورینام |
| Uruguay | orogue | اوروگوئه |

| Ecuador | ekvādor | اکوادور |
| The Bahamas | bāhāmā | باهاما |
| Haiti | hāiti | هائیتی |

| Dominican Republic | jomhuri-ye dominikan | جمهوری دومینیکن |
| Panama | pānāmā | پاناما |
| Jamaica | jāmāikā | جامائیکا |

## 153. Africa

| Egypt | mesr | مصر |
| Morocco | marākeš | مراکش |
| Tunisia | tunes | تونس |

| Ghana | qanā | غنا |
| Zanzibar | zangbār | زنگبار |
| Kenya | keniyā | کنیا |
| Libya | libi | لیبی |
| Madagascar | mādāgāskār | ماداگاسکار |

| Namibia | nāmibiyā | نامیبیا |
| Senegal | senegāl | سنگال |
| Tanzania | tānzāniyā | تانزانیا |
| South Africa | jomhuri-ye āfriqā-ye jonubi | جمهوری آفریقای جنوبی |

## 154. Australia. Oceania

| Australia | ostorāliyā | استرالیا |
| New Zealand | niyuzland | نیوزلند |

| Tasmania | tāsmāni | تاسمانی |
| French Polynesia | polinezi-ye farānse | پلینزی فرانسه |

## 155. Cities

| Amsterdam | āmesterdām | آمستردام |
| Ankara | ānkārā | آنکارا |
| Athens | āten | آتن |
| Baghdad | baqdād | بغداد |
| Bangkok | bānkok | بانکوک |

| Barcelona | bārselon | بارسلون |
| Beijing | pekan | پکن |
| Beirut | beyrut | بیروت |
| Berlin | berlin | برلین |
| Bonn | bon | بن |

| Bordeaux | bordo | بوردو |
| Bratislava | bratislav | براتیسلاو |
| Brussels | boruksel | بروکسل |
| Bucharest | boxārest | بخارست |
| Budapest | budāpest | بوداپست |
| Cairo | qāhere | قاهره |

| Chicago | šikāgo | شیکاگو |
| Copenhagen | kopenhāk | کپنهاک |
| Dar-es-Salaam | dārossalām | دارالسلام |
| Delhi | dehli | دهلی |
| Dubai | debi | دبی |

| Dublin | dublin | دوبلین |
| Düsseldorf | duseldorf | دوسلدورف |
| Florence | felorāns | فلورانس |
| Frankfurt | ferānkfort | فرانکفورت |
| Geneva | ženev | ژنو |

| Hamburg | hāmborg | هامبورگ |
| Hanoi | hānoy | هانوی |
| Havana | hāvānā | هاوانا |
| Helsinki | helsinki | هلسینکی |
| Hiroshima | hirošimā | هیروشیما |

| Hong Kong | hong kong | هنگ کنگ |
| Istanbul | estānbol | استامبول |
| Jerusalem | beytolmoqaddas | بیت المقدس |
| Kolkata (Calcutta) | kalkate | کلکته |
| Kuala Lumpur | kuālālāmpur | کوالالامپور |

| Kyiv | keyf | کیف |
| Lisbon | lisbun | لیسبون |
| London | landan | لندن |
| Los Angeles | losānjeles | لس آنجلس |
| Lyons | liyon | لیون |
| Madrid | mādrid | مادرید |

| Marseille | mārsey | مارسی |
| Mexico City | mekziko | مکزیکو |
| Miami | mayāmey | میامی |
| Montreal | montreāl | مونترآل |
| Moscow | moskow | مسکو |

| Mumbai (Bombay) | bombai | بمبئی |
| Munich | munix | مونیخ |
| Nairobi | nāyrubi | نایروبی |
| Naples | nāpl | ناپل |
| New York | niyuyork | نیویورک |

| Nice | nis | نیس |
| Oslo | oslo | اسلو |

| Ottawa | otāvā | اتاوا |
| Paris | pāris | پاریس |
| Prague | perāg | پراگ |

| Rio de Janeiro | riyo-do-žāniro | ریو دو ژانیرو |
| Rome | ram | رم |
| Saint Petersburg | sān peterzburg | سن پترزبورگ |
| Seoul | seul | سئول |
| Shanghai | šānghāy | شانگهای |

| Singapore | sangāpur | سنگاپور |
| Stockholm | āstokholm | استکهلم |
| Sydney | sidni | سیدنی |
| Taipei | tāype | تایپه |
| The Hague | lāhe | لاهه |
| Tokyo | tokiyo | توکیو |

| Toronto | torento | تورنتو |
| Venice | veniz | ونیز |
| Vienna | viyan | وین |
| Warsaw | varšow | ورشو |
| Washington | vāšangton | واشنگتن |